CW00666533

ABYEI OF THE NGOK DINKA

ABYEI OF THE NGOK DINKA

NOT YET SOUTH SUDAN

by Bona Malwal

Bourchier

© Bona Malwal

First edition published in 2017

The right of Bona Malwal to be identified as the author of this work has been asserted by the author in accordance with the Copyright, Designs and Patent Act 1988.

British Library Cataloguing in Publication Data
Data available

Library of Congress Cataloging in Publication Data
Data available

Typeset by Mach 3 Solutions Ltd

Printed in Great Britain by CPI Anthony Rowe

ISBN 978-0-9934692-6-8

To my Twic Mayardit community of Greater Gogrial district of
Greater Bahr el Ghazal province of South Sudan

Acknowledgement

I am fortunate to have a colleague here, at St Antony's College of the University of Oxford, who has been very helpful in typing all my recent manuscripts. It is, therefore, with deep appreciation and delight that I acknowledge the help of Mrs Caroline Davis who typed this manuscript in her own time outside of her work at the College – with speed, diligence and personal dedication.

Contents

Preface

'Any intelligent fool can make things bigger, more complex and more violent. It takes a touch of genius, and a lot of courage, to move in the opposite direction.'

Albert Einstein

This account of events that relate to the Ngok Dinka people of Abyei of Southern Kordofan in the Republic of Sudan (Northern Sudan) is a personal narrative. It is not a work that has arisen from academic or intellectual research, but describes events that I witnessed first hand. My own life and that of my family have been close to the Ngok Dinka people. At one time, before the traditional leadership of the Ngok decided to lead their community to Kordofan in Northern Sudan, my own section, known as Kuac Madut Ring – after my father, Madut Ring, who became the first chief of Kuac Anganya – refused to join the Ngok to become part of Northern Sudan.

My father and Chief Deng Majok Kuol Arop of the Ngok Dinka people of Abyei were contemporaries, being initiated (head marked) on the same day to be recognized as Dinka adults.

The departure of the Ngok people to Kordofan left the Kuac people of Twic in South Sudan without a chiefdom of their own, something my father struggled for. Finally it was granted, but by this time the national politics of Sudan had become unstable, with South Sudan and Northern Sudan enmeshed in a war of independence.

The North had inherited political power from the British, who had been the colonial power over the whole of Sudan – South and North – for more than sixty years. The Ngok people of Abyei were always represented in the political and military struggle of South Sudan against the North – even though, in the earlier years, there was no clear political definition of the struggle. Did South Sudan just want to run its own affairs under a still united Sudan or did the South want to separate from the North to form an independent country?

As this book reveals, when the South decided to call for self-determination I had come of age and was one of the political leaders of South Sudan who was advocating this right. As a founder and first secretary-general of the Southern Front, the first populist intellectual political movement of South Sudan, this remained my stance throughout my political career, which naturally made me a political enemy of those who recognized that self-determination for the South would leave an area such as Abyei, together with its entire Ngok Dinka population, in Northern Sudan. The proponents of self-determination for the South, such as myself, had to oppose those who were advocating a united Sudan, a stance that was being articulated by, among others, the late Colonel John Garang de Mabior (1945–2005), leader of the newest liberation movement for South Sudan at the time, the Sudan People's Liberation Army (SPLA).

The SPLA's desire for a united Sudan had attracted fighters from the neighbouring marginalized regions of Northern Sudan, such as Abyei, the Nuba Mountains and the Angesina people of Southern Blue Nile. Fighters from these marginalized Northern Sudanese communities, with racial affinity to South Sudan, joined the SPLA to fight for a united Sudan. I became a target for these groups for daring to continue to advocate self-determination for the South despite the leadership of the 'Revolution' deciding that the country had to remain one Sudan.

The Dinka Ngok leaders of the SPLA took matters much further when it came to Colonel Garang's opponents. It became clear that even violent acts such as lynching one of his opponents would endear them to him. I became a target, not only for political and social character assassination, but also for physical elimination.

I have described in this book the relationship between the Dinka people of Abyei and Kordofan, their provinces, and between the causes of the people of South Sudan and Abyei. I decided that I would no longer be part of whatever the political leadership of Abyei wanted to do to find a solution to an intricate problem, made more complicated by the behaviour of the Ngok leadership of the ruling party in South

Sudan's government, who still believe that only by another war with Northern Sudan can the problem be resolved.

The leadership of the ruling party in South Sudan has also abetted the failure of Sudan to find a solution to the Abyei problem, by refusing to confront the Ngok leadership of Abyei with the hard facts of why Abyei is not and should never be a cause of conflict between Khartoum and Juba – as the facts presented here indicate. Moreover, when Juba packs its government with politicians from Abyei – who then command the army of South Sudan, the SPLA, with generals from Abyei – Khartoum only perceives war with the South over Abyei, and not peace.

A solution to the problem of the Ngok people of Abyei will only come about if the political life of South Sudan is freed from the influence of the leaders of Abyei, and when the foreign friends of South Sudan are no longer misled into believing that Abyei is a disputed territory between Northern Sudan and South Sudan. The story of how Abyei and its people, the Ngok Dinka, became part of Northern Sudan has been distorted, and therefore the solution to the problem has become more complicated.

Finally, in my view, the solution to the problem lies in the implementation of the Abyei protocol of the Comprehensive Peace Agreement (CPA). This calls for a referendum in Abyei, in which the Ngok people of Abyei can freely decide whether to remain in Northern Sudan, because, legally, at the time of writing they are still part of Northern Sudan, in accordance with the borders defined on 1 January 1956, when Sudan became independent from Britain. This will remain the case until the vote takes place.

The 2011 referendum, which made South Sudan independent on 9 July of that year, was conducted on the basis of these borders. It is in the best interests of everyone, especially the Ngok Dinka people of Abyei and their leadership, to submit to the terms of the Abyei protocol.

The present regime in Khartoum is the one that signed the CPA with the South in 2005; it has fully accepted the terms of the CPA and has recognized the independence of South Sudan. There is every reason to believe that the regime will also respect the outcome of an Abyei referendum if it is conducted freely and fairly with its cooperation and participation. This is the only possible peaceful outcome for the Abyei problem. Anything else would be a dangerous bluff, and South Sudan, having won its independence under the peaceful terms of the CPA, must not become part of such a bluff, which would not bring peace to the Ngok people of Abyei or even to South Sudan itself.

Abbreviations

AU	African Union
CPA	Comprehensive Peace Agreement
CSI	Christian Solidarity International
ICC	International Criminal Court
IGAD	Intergovernmental Authority on Development
NCP	National Congress Party
NIF	National Islamic Front
OAU	Organization of African Unity
OLS	Operation Lifeline Sudan
SANU	Sudan African National Union
SPLA	Sudan People's Liberation Army
SPLM	Sudan People's Liberation Movement
SSU	Sudan Socialist Union

Introduction

The Ngok Dinka people of Abyei of Southern Kordofan in Northern Sudan have found themselves, through no fault of their own, in what until now has been an irresolvable situation. Since 1905 they have been part of the Northern Sudanese colonial province of Kordofan, first under the British colonial authority and then through the insistence of their own ethnic leaders. Many activists involved in the problem of Abyei – as it has become known – seek to blame one side or the other for the Ngok Dinka's terrible predicament. This extremely small territory is currently neither part of Northern Sudan – since 9 July 2011 a separate country from South Sudan – nor part of South Sudan. The Northern Sudanese ethnic community, the Messiria Baggara Arabs, which disputes the area with the Ngok Dinka community of Abyei, does not want to recognize the possibility that the Ngok Dinka territory belongs to the Ngok and not to them.

I have decided to write about this problem not just because I come from the area immediately south of Abyei, in South Sudan, but also because I share a close affinity with the Ngok people and understand why they find themselves in their current predicament.

The leaders of the Ngok Dinka community of Abyei have publicly and repeatedly accused me of being partly responsible for Abyei being in Northern Sudan, when the small territory should be part of South Sudan. I therefore owe it to posterity, to the facts of history and to myself, to relate this sad history from my point of view.

The current situation is the result of shared mistakes that are not, unfortunately, taken into account by those who think they have a duty and responsibility to resolve the Abyei problem. It is the contention of this book that those dealing with the Abyei situation need to take the historical facts into account in order to arrive at a solution. Believing that one group has the power and ability to overcome the other is what has led the Ngok Dinka people into today's state of affairs.

The difficulty in resolving the situation has now become much more complicated, not only because South Sudan is today an independent state, but because the local leaders of South Sudan's ruling party, the Sudan People's Liberation Movement (SPLM) from Abyei, have a notion that there is some invincible power that will drive their people back to the South from Northern Sudan.

When the aspiring leadership of South Sudan – of which I was a member – first raised the political slogan for self-determination for South Sudan in the early 1960s, they needed to define the border between themselves and Northern Sudan. The natural and easy choice was to adopt the existing provincial colonial borders – a clever tactical political move that denied the Northern Sudanese politicians a chance to dispute them. When the British first ruled Sudan – for more than sixty years from the 1820s – the country was split into nine provinces: six provinces in Northern Sudan and three provinces in South Sudan. These boundaries placed Abyei in Northern Sudan, in line with the wishes of the local Ngok Dinka leadership of the time.

As the independence of Sudan from Britain became inevitable, the British colonial authorities tried very hard to persuade the Ngok leadership to return to South Sudan, because it was obvious that even if South Sudan had to remain permanently part of Northern Sudan, a small Ngok Dinka community of Abyei would be totally marginalized in Kordofan, the province of Northern Sudan to which the Ngok leadership wanted their people to belong. Now, with South Sudan an independent country, the Abyei situation has become incredibly difficult to resolve, with the only chance for its resolution depending entirely on the Sudan government in Khartoum and the government of an independent South Sudan in Juba not only agreeing to a solution, but also sticking to the original agreement about Abyei that they made.

The Comprehensive Peace Agreement (CPA), which both Khartoum and Juba seem to hold to, and which is the basis on which South Sudan is now an independent state, has an independent protocol on Abyei. This says that the Ngok Dinka people of Abyei should decide in a free referendum, in which only they can vote, whether to return to South Sudan or remain in the North.

Conducting this Abyei referendum has become very complicated because relations between Khartoum and Juba have deteriorated so far that the victims of hostilities – in areas such as Abyei, whose problem should have been resolved amicably long before South Sudan broke away from the North – do not seem to have a future.

It was to resolve problems between Northern Sudan and South Sudan that the CPA established an interim period lasting six years. During this period, for example, the Abyei referendum could be conducted on the future of this small area, which currently dominates hostilities between the two nations. It is important to note that, in spite of the independence of South Sudan from the North, both countries still need one another in order to survive as viable states. Abyei must not be allowed to become a perpetual spoiler.

For more than a hundred years, the Ngok Dinka people of Abyei have been administered as part of the Southern Kordofan region of the colonial province of Kordofan. This was a shared decision by the colonial authorities in what was known as Anglo-Egyptian Sudan, and the independent Republic of Sudan after 1 January 1956. The Ngok Dinka of Abyei acquiesced with the decision to annex them to Northern Sudan, even if they did not accept it wholeheartedly – because no decision, colonial or otherwise, was taken during the colonial era without reason, whether good or bad.

Central to the original British colonial decision to annex the Abyei area to Kordofan was the issue of livestock grazing and water for the Messiria Baggara Arabs. The British sought to provide the Arabs with some pasture and water, especially during the dry season, when their semi-desert territory becomes barren. This lasts from October for four to six months. To persuade the Dinka community to allow this was difficult, as they did not like certain aspects of the Arabs' cultural behaviours, and could not permit them to be practised within their territory. The British, therefore, sought to make it known to the Dinka that they had no choice in the matter. Naming the River Kiir with an Arabic name, as the Arab River, the British thought, was the only way to make the Dinka at least accept the sharing of the waters and the pasture close to the borders of the South and the North.

When the British colonial authorities started to undertake this rather difficult administrative jigsaw, the area on the border between Kordofan in Northern Sudan and the Dinka area of Northern Bahr el Ghazal was often flooded during the rainy season, and remained wet with good grazing pasture throughout much of the dry season, nearly until the next rains. The Baggara Arabs, therefore, did not need to penetrate too far into Dinka country to find water and pasture. As drought entered the picture, though, the British were forced to encroach deeper into Dinka territory to solve the Baggara Arabs' grazing problems.

Mistakes were made as the colonial authorities surveyed the border areas in order to demarcate the pasture and water. When the first border surveys were conducted, during the rainy season, British surveyors erroneously gave the name Bahr el Arab to a group of small water-courses north of the Kiir. When these smaller rivers dried up before the end of the dry season, and the Baggara Arabs had to migrate further south in search of water and pasture, the British renamed the River Kiir as Bahr el Arab.

However, the Baggara Arabs' search for water and pasture did not only affect Kordofan. The same problem was encountered between the Malual Dinka of Mading Aweil of Northern Bahr el Ghazal, further west on the River Kiir, and the Rezeigat Baggara Arabs of Southern Darfur. In fact, this border was much longer and affected the Dinka more deeply. Since the Rezeigat Arabs were much more numerous than the Messiria Baggara Arabs, and had many more cattle, the British colonial authorities encroached further into Dinka territory here. The British named all that pasture south of the River Kiir, south of Safah, between Aweil and el Daien in Southern Darfur, as an Arab pasture. The Dinka of Aweil did not agree to this, and at the time of writing the problem is still one of the border issues to be resolved between Northern Sudan and South Sudan.

In view of the intricate political situation summarized above, Arop Biong had to act skilfully. Rather than create a perpetual situation of war between the Ngok Dinka and the Messiria Baggara Arabs, and realizing he could not escape the Arab encroachment, he decided to seek the colonial authority's approval to have his people treated as part of Kordofan province. The British accepted the wisdom of this idea, and so from 1905 Abyei became part of the Kordofan – and therefore of Northern Sudan.

In South Sudan, however, political enlightenment and awareness had been developing, something which the British colonial powers had done nothing to stop during their sixty years of rule over the country. It was against this backdrop that the South Sudanese triggered a revolution of a sort in August 1955, during which some of the educated sons of the Ngok Dinka of Abyei looked to South Sudan both for political support and absorption. The result of this was that over time much of the elite of the Ngok Dinka of Abyei began to look south for inspiration and for salvation. This was the true beginning of the suffering of the ordinary Ngok Dinka people. The North would not accept that the people of Abyei could migrate to South Sudan, even if that was what the Ngok people actually wanted.

On their part, the educated Ngok Dinka people of Abyei have made their own mistakes and miscalculations, as discussed in this book. This makes it extremely difficult to resolve the Abyei question, a problem that, unlike the separation of South Sudan from Northern Sudan, cannot be resolved through war, but only by pursuing peace negotiations.

It took me more than two decades, during the latest part of the liberation struggle of the people of South Sudan, to finally decide that I should write this account, which includes what I know personally about the case of the Ngok Dinka of Abyei. Why was this so? I hope that the reader will find out the answer in the story that follows.

The Ngok Dinka of Abyei are as close to me as it is possible to be. Before the Ngok leaders decided that they and their people should be administered as part of the Kordofan province of Northern Sudan, long before colonialism had decided to annex South Sudan to Northern Sudan, to form what became the colonial state of Sudan, the leading Ngok family of Arop Biong concluded that it was in the best interests of their people, the Ngok Dinka of Abyei, to be administered as part of Kordofan. Kordofan, Darfur and Blue Nile are the three provinces of Northern Sudan that border the two provinces of South Sudan – Bahr el Ghazal and Upper Nile.

Before the dawn of chiefdom in the Dinka community, both the Ngok Dinka of Abyei and my ancestral section, Kuac Anganya, were loosely one cultural section of the Dinka. The leaders and the elders of Kuac Anganya decided against joining the Ngok and being administered as part of Kordofan, therefore becoming Northern Sudanese. That decision by six sub-sections of Kuac Anganya caused them to face torment from the British colonial administration. Rather than leaving the six Kuac sections alone under their own chiefdom, they were split into two: one sub-chiefdom, the Anganya section, was annexed to Amuol of Chief Bol Chol Nyuol. The other five sections – Aher, Ayuang, Jur Bou, Guot Juor and Ator – were annexed to Akwar of Juk Chom.

The leaders of Kuac Anganya were never content with their lot, and they continued to complain, appealing to be allowed to form their own chiefdom. There followed a long struggle, led by their own chief alongside my father, Chief Madut Ring, who was the sub-chief of Aher, one of the other five Kuac sections. My father was appointed deputy head chief of the entire section of Akwar, to which they were now annexed. This section remained known as Akwar; but my father and his sub-chiefs never relented, continuing to campaign for their own chiefdom.

The Kuac Anganya demand for their own chiefdom under my father became so forceful that the last British district commissioner of Gogrial, Ranald Boyle (Tim Atiep), to whom I became a close personal friend, used to refer to my father as a tireless rebel whenever his name came up in conversation. It was during the Sudan People's Liberation Army (SPLA)'s war of liberation in 1983–2005 that Kuac Anganya was finally allowed to become an independent chiefdom under my father and finally gained a new name: Kuac Madut Ring. My father did not live much longer after this, having been a struggling chief since the 1930s, and he died of natural causes at his cattle camp in 1997. He was replaced by his son, the current chief Wundit Madut Ring, who was one of his nearly thirty sons fighting within the SPLA to liberate South Sudan from the North. Chief Wundit Madut Ring was an intelligence officer in the SPLA under the command of General Daniel Awet Akot, who was gracious enough to release him so he could take over the chiefdom.

How the decision by the chief of the Ngok Dinka of Abyei to become part of Northern Sudan came about has been subject to much political distortion. By 1952, it had become clear to the British colonial officials of South Sudan that the Ngok Dinka would not fare well in Northern Sudan. The final attempt to return the Ngok to the South was made at a huge conference at Abyei town in February–March 1952. All the Dinka chiefs from the Dinka districts of Bahr el Ghazal and Upper Nile were invited. My father took me along with him to witness this meeting, instead of spending my long annual vacation at the cattle camp, as I usually did. I was in Bussere Intermediate School (junior secondary school) at this time.

The meeting did not convince Chief Deng Majok Kuol Arop to return his people to the South. But before the South articulated its own political demand – for independence from the North – the people of Abyei did not fare as badly as they did later, when South Sudan decided that its political future could not be the same as that of Northern Sudan, whose leading Islamic Arab cultural group had no thought of accommodating other religions or other cultures, or sharing political power with any non-Arab or non-Muslim people.

As the political cause for South Sudan began to be more widely articulated, the educated and enlightened Ngok Dinka community of Abyei split into two, between those who wanted to join the South and those who wanted to continue in the North. Thus the real plight of the Ngok Dinka of Abyei became confused, if not lost altogether.

The SPLA, which was now joined by a score of educated Ngok Dinka, did not help matters, in that its articulation of the cause of the war of liberation for South Sudan became confused between the liberation of the whole of the Sudan under the banner of 'New Sudan' and a total liberation of South Sudan.

Other political events, before the foundation of the SPLA and since, have combined to distort the political cause of the people of Abyei, and have made the resolution of this conflict much more difficult to achieve. The Ngok elite, largely members of the ruling Kuol Arop family, have not helped the cause, and their continuing strong influence on the politics of South Sudan is not assisting the people of Abyei.

Realistically, the only credible solution to the Abyei situation depends on the cooperation of the two governments, in Khartoum and in Juba. However, the SPLM's attitude to political problems, even to domestic political problems, is to use force before anything else. Without Khartoum and Juba seeing eye to eye on how to solve the Abyei predicament, it is almost impossible to conceive of a solution. Yet Khartoum sees the strong political and administrative influence wielded by the Ngok elite within the government of South Sudan as tantamount to a war council in Juba. The story that follows gives some instances of undue intransigence on the part of those whose best way out of the Abyei problem ought to be political understanding, and cooperation with Khartoum.

The Abyei case cannot be resolved by military force. The leadership of South Sudan, including the leaders of the small Ngok Dinka community of Abyei, ought to accept, for whatever it is worth, that Abyei is for now part of Kordofan, a province of Northern Sudan, according to the 1956 demarcation and the pre-1956 demarcation. If they had been well accommodated by the North, politically and socially, or if South Sudan had not broken away from the North, the territory of Abyei would be part of Northern Sudan. No one, neither the people of Abyei on their own nor the people of South Sudan, has claimed that a change of borders should take place in order to make the Ngok people become Sudanese. Geographically, if not culturally, the Ngok Dinka people of Abyei had been Northern Sudanese long before Sudan became independent.

It is the maltreatment of the Ngok people by their neighbours, the Messiria Baggara Arabs, and the political upheaval between Northern Sudan and South Sudan that demands political resolution, since the assumption is that the majority of the Ngok people want to revert to South Sudan. For reasons stated in this book, if they remain in Northern Sudan their future is precarious.

No one wants to draw borders on the basis of ethnicity or race. There is no country in the world that is one race or one ethnic group. If a country decides to break up into two separate independent states, in the way that Northern Sudan and South Sudan have done, then groups or even sections of groups can choose to become a part of one of the two countries because of their political circumstances.

The Ngok people of Abyei were always a front-line community, as far as relations between Northern Sudan and South Sudan were concerned. That is why the negotiations between the government in Khartoum and the SPLM rightly concluded that the Ngok people of Abyei should be consulted in a separate referendum, so they could choose whether or not to remain in Northern Sudan or revert to South Sudan. The Abyei protocol is part of the peace settlement between Northern Sudan and South Sudan and needs to be carried out, no matter how delayed it might be. There are a few other matters besides the Abyei protocol, also decided at the 2005 peace agreement, which have not yet been carried out. These need to be acted upon, because it is after the implementation of these things, followed by the border demarcation and the full resolution of outstanding security issues relating to the peace agreement, that there will finally be peace between the Republic of Sudan (Northern Sudan) and South Sudan.

There have, of course, been regrettable mistakes made by both signatories to the 2005 peace agreement, and these make resolution of the Abyei issue contentious. Yet we have to remember that the problem of Abyei is not a dispute between Northern Sudan and South Sudan. It never was and should never have been allowed to become so. The political awakening of South Sudan brought with it the realization that the Ngok people of Abyei had been part of Northern Sudan since 1905 – and this is a fact that no one can dispute.

This political awakening began with the 1947 Juba conference, when the British colonial powers decided to annex South Sudan to Northern Sudan to create a single country. Abyei was already in the North, and had been since 1905; the South had never laid claim to it. On the contrary, when the South decided to demand the right of self-determination, from March 1965 onwards, it did not make claims to areas that were culturally and ethnically akin to South Sudan, such as Abyei for instance.

The South demanded that the geographical South Sudan should be considered as defined by the borders of the three Southern provinces of Bahr el Ghazal, Equatoria and Upper Nile. It is the strong influence of the Ngok leaders of the SPLM on the contemporary politics of South Sudan that has complicated the problem of the Ngok people of Abyei, because the leaders treated the territory as a disputed area. The people of South Sudan had never laid claim to Abyei. If there is anything that political South Sudan has done that could be defined as interference in the affairs of Abyei, it is allowing members of the Ngok community of Abyei to become part of the political liberation movement of South Sudan.

No government of South Sudan should claim any people from its neighbouring countries just on the basis of shared ethnicity. This is a policy that would set South Sudan at odds with all its neighbours. The Organization of African Unity (OAU), the mother organization of the independent countries of Africa to which the Republic of South Sudan – at the time of writing, the youngest nation of the world – belongs, foresaw the danger of claiming communities belonging to other countries on ethnic affinity when it ruled in its founding charter that Africa must not tamper with colonial African borders based on ethnicity claims. If the OAU reneged on this principle of sacrosanct colonial borders to accommodate the new state of South Sudan in accordance with the terms of the CPA, it was as a way of bringing peace to a long-time war-torn Sudan. South Sudan must not tamper with the long-held OAU principle of sacrosanct colonial borders, except for those defined by the CPA – for example in conducting the Abyei referendum under the CPA and recognizing the outcome of that referendum as part of the CPA peace process of 2005.

South Sudan, Africa's newest nation state, has shown how fragile it is. It must be extremely careful about making border claims on the basis of ethnic affinity, and should not render itself suspect by its many neighbours. South Sudan has shared ethnicities on its eastern borders with Ethiopia, with whom it shares the Nuer and the Anyuak; with Kenya and Uganda to the south, with whom it shares the Turkana, the Acholi, the Madi, the Kakua, for example; with the Democratic Republic of the Congo and the Central African Republic to the west, with whom it shares the large Zande ethnic group over an impossible-to-manage border. That the ruling party of South Sudan, the SPLM, refuses to control and manage the behaviour of some of its own leaders, including the leaders of the Abyei community, is a clear source of concern when it comes to the potential for conflict with these neighbours.

The CPA Abyei protocol is very clear. It says that the Ngok people should be consulted in a peaceful referendum – one person one vote – to decide whether or not they want to become citizens of South Sudan instead of citizens of Northern Sudan. But the Abyei leaders of the SPLM have contributed to making this a cause of dispute between Khartoum and Juba, instead of using it as a point of cooperation and agreeing how to resolve the matter.

As previously mentioned, the SPLM has compounded the mistake by making its members from Abyei the principal rulers of South Sudan and giving commanders of the SPLA leadership of the army of South Sudan. This army has already attempted to take over Abyei by force of arms, even before the result of the impending Abyei referendum is known. Attempts to annex Abyei to South Sudan by force have clearly complicated the issue. At the time of writing, the SPLA has been expelled from Abyei three times. If Northern Sudan refuses to recognize and honour the outcome of the referendum, the South and the Ngok people would be entitled to recourse to another type of action, although the viability of military action over Abyei is not clear.

Then there is a more serious mistake that has been made by the Abyei leaders of the SPLM. Many South Sudanese already resent the fact that the Ngok leaders are also the rulers of South Sudan. When the struggle for power in South Sudan erupted between the leaders of the SPLM, the leaders of Abyei stood accused of having sided with the SPLM rebels, who wanted to overthrow the elected government of South Sudan by force of arms. All this has created an excuse for Khartoum to refuse to cooperate with Juba on resolving the Abyei problem. This internal power struggle within South Sudan has put back by many years, if not decades, any efforts to resolve the Abyei problem through a referendum.

The small Ngok Dinka community of Abyei currently finds itself carrying a much larger burden in the deteriorating relationship between the young Republic of South Sudan and Northern Sudan, through no fault of the Ngok people as a community. This is because the land of Ngok is wedged between the Dinka as a whole, most of which is now the independent Republic of South Sudan, and the Messiria Baggara Arabs of Southern Kordofan, a nomadic community. The River Kiir, the main provider of water and pasture for both the Baggara Arabs and the Dinka, now forms the border between Northern Sudan and Southern Sudan at this point.

It is impossible to determine who owns the River Kiir and who does not, because it is a source of livelihood for much of the dry season, and those who live in communities on both sides of the border must find a way to share the water and the pasture. No one, since the creation of man, has ever had the right to deny another man the means of liveli-hood. Nature does not accept it and human beings themselves do not accept it. This is why, with the advancement of civilization and human understanding, there are now humanitarian laws that provide sanctuary to refugees who have crossed from their legitimate homes to another person's legitimate home.

Once the British colonial administration had determined access to the River Kiir, and renamed it, enforcement was not difficult – and it would appear that the Arop Biong family, the ruling family of the Ngok Dinka people of Abyei, saw the difficulties their people would face if they ignored the colonial decision. However, their people could not be separated from the river nor could they lose their land, which lies north of the river, to the Arabs. It seemed clear to them that the Arabs would never claim just the pasture along the River Kiir. Now the Dinka river had become Arab, together with the territory along it, the Arop Biong family decided that the Ngok Dinka section should be annexed to Southern Kordofan and treated as part of the Kordofan province of Northern Sudan, rather than as part of Bahr el Ghazal, one of the three British colonial provinces of South Sudan. Was this a right or a wrong decision?

There is a debate raging, not only within the Ngok community of Abyei, about what turned out to be a colossal mistake. Was it the fault of Arop Biong himself, or his son, Kuol Arop Biong, or his grandson, Deng Majok Kuol Arop, and his children? Whatever is the case, the decision has cost the Ngok people very dearly, because of the weak political leadership of Sudan and mismanagement after the British left.

It is obvious, though, that while the Arop Biong family was influ-ential, it cannot be held responsible on its own. The decision was confirmed and reinforced over the years by those who followed, by the leadership and indeed by much of the Ngok population.

Chief Deng Majok Kuol Arop is credited above anyone else with keeping the Ngok people in the North, for reasons of personal benefit. These accusations have been strongly fortified by the debate about the future position of the Ngok people of Abyei, and the debate itself has become part of the political enlightenment and awakening that has graced the whole country since independence.

Now that South Sudan has attained its independence, as a result of a very long and a bloody armed struggle, the future of the Ngok people of Abyei has become the subject of a heated debate, which is regrettably not being conducted prudently. Many parties are responsible for this. There has been a notable failure by the leadership of South Sudan to make it clear to the SPLM leadership that, as far as South Sudan is concerned, Abyei will remain part of Northern Sudan until the Ngok people of Abyei have voted. Without the decision of the Ngok people of Abyei, in a free vote that is recognized by both sides, they cannot be saved from the catastrophe in which they find themselves.

This writer pleads guilty for calling at the 1965 Round Table Conference in Khartoum between the South and the North for the right of South Sudan to self-determination, which has successfully resulted in an independent South Sudan without Abyei. As one of the founders and architects of this, I was very much part of the decisions that confirmed the borders of South Sudan and Northern Sudan – decisions that did not deliberately intend to neglect the cause of the Ngok people of Abyei but were looking at the larger picture. It should now be clear to all concerned that had the Southern Front not confined the borders to those of the three provinces of colonial South Sudan and the six provinces of Northern Sudan, perhaps the debate about self-determination would have raged on until today without resolution. This might have pleased the North, which would perhaps never have accepted the demarcation of any new borders between South and North.

Members of the CPA of 2005 between the South and the North will know exactly what I am talking about here. Without border demarcation, the South could not have carried out that famous referendum on self-determination which, of course, has resulted in an independent republic today. Whatever pain this inflicts, South Sudan is still an independent country. There may be those who regret what the South is doing to itself, but to me it is part of the price of freedom.

With the Abyei people clearly in mind, the Addis Ababa Peace Agreement of 1972 referred to communities with affinity to the South, to allow them to decide to return to the South in a referendum. That Agreement was not as solid a peace agreement as the CPA of 2005. That is why, in May 1983, Jaafar Mohamed Nimeiri tampered with the Agreement – an act that South Sudan should perhaps not regret, because Nimeiri's recklessness led to the CPA, and this resulted in an independent South Sudan.

The difficulties for any leader of South Sudan regarding Abyei have long been present. Colonel John Garang de Mabior, the late leader of the SPLM, and the final negotiator of the 2005 peace agreement with Northern Sudan, had to consider what to do about Abyei, the Nuba Mountains region, Southern Kordofan and the Southern Blue Nile region of the Angesina people. With the help of international mediators, who aided him in bringing about the 2005 peace agreement between the South and the North, Garang negotiated the protocols for Abyei and the other two regions of the North. These protocols provide for the parties to consult the communities of these three regions to discover what they want.

Had he known the facts of the political situation, Colonel Garang would have handled these matters in a much more straightforward way. But, of course, he is no longer with us, and given the lack of discipline that has afflicted his movement after his death, it is not possible to conceive of a solution to the Abyei predicament unless discipline returns to the SPLM and it speaks with one voice about the political and social problems currently being faced.

It is unfortunate that the leaders of Abyei within the SPLM are amongst the most undisciplined leaders in South Sudan. They behave as if they are already part of South Sudan – indeed the country's legitimate leaders. Not only that, they have spread themselves into the many feuding factions of the SPLM, and, looking down the barrel of a gun, are now vying for power in South Sudan. More than that, they behave as if only they can solve any problem facing South Sudan today. This not only makes it impossible for them to gain sympathy for the cause of Abyei, but also creates rivalry with other leaders of South Sudan.

This leaves the cause of the people of Abyei on the sidelines, as their leaders are struggling for power that is not yet theirs. Who wants to help a rival to succeed, not only in terms of political power but also wealth? This describes the politics of South Sudan today.

The Abyei problem is one of the most potent causes of conflict between the South Sudan and Northern Sudan, and will remain so for the foreseeable future. Khartoum now believes that the Abyei situation is not an issue in which they should be involved. They regard the Abyei problem as a cause for war between them and Juba, not amenable to cooperation or peace. It is thus difficult to foresee a solution that will relieve the people of Abyei and normalize relations between the two countries.

Colonel Garang's view of the situation in Abyei and the two other marginalized areas of central Sudan, the Nuba Mountains and the Angesina Hills, was to use these flashpoints as places of contact and cooperation, rather than arenas in which war should be perpetuated. Garang was a leader who had toiled for the idea of unity between South Sudan and Northern Sudan, which was why he named his movement for the liberation of the whole of Sudan, instead of confining it to South Sudan. Yet he had to submit to the practical political reality of Sudan and reduce his ambition to liberate the whole of Sudan to achieving, instead, only the aspirations of the people of South Sudan.

If the inheritors of Garang's broader vision – achieving peace and tranquillity in the whole of Sudan – had a wide political vision of their own, it would be possible to achieve the aspirations of the people of Abyei, whatever they may be: either becoming part of the now independent South Sudan or remaining in the North. Either of these two outcomes could have helped to achieve peace and tranquillity between the two Sudans, if not unity.

The idea that leaders of a small territory such as Abyei, with such a small population, would nominate themselves as the perpetuators of war between the South and the North of Sudan is truly mind-boggling.

These are people who should be advocates of peace between the two countries at all times, because that is the most comfortable position to hold, for them and for their people. Any advocacy for war, as is the policy of the Ngok leaders of the SPLM, leads to where Abyei and its people are today.

Advocating international intervention, of the type that now leaves the very small area of Abyei under the protection of an Ethiopian peacekeeping force of the United Nations, the African Union and the Intergovernmental Authority on Development (IGAD), means that no space is left which the Ngok people can call their own. How long do the SPLM leaders of Ngok think this situation can go on for? Clearly, this joint African Union–United Nations peacekeeping force is only tolerated by one side of the Abyei conflict, the government of South Sudan, which is heavily influenced by the Ngok leaders of the SPLM. On the northern side, the situation in Abyei, involving a foreign force and without a peace agreement, is not acceptable. Insecurity in Abyei is clearly being provoked by Khartoum through the use of the armed Messiria Baggara Arab militia. Abyei's local civilians now live in a heavily militarized area – but is such a small civilian population worth the substantial foreign militarization?

The current leaders of the SPLM, now the rulers of South Sudan, are influencing government policy in a way that will never lead to peace in Abyei. I am concerned by this, because anything that touches the Ngok people of Abyei automatically touches me and my people. It is almost impossible to separate the Ngok Kuol Arop people of Abyei from the people of Kuac Madut Ring, or from the larger Twic Mayardit community, which I have had the honour of representing in political leadership for at least fifty years.

The River Kiir crosses the whole of Twic Mayardit, from west to east. It is Twic Mayardit that has borne the brunt of the calamity.

As a community, Kuac Madut Ring has been close to the Ngok people of Abyei since time immemorial, both culturally and spiritually. In the old days, before the country became spoiled by wars, annual worship of the shared spirits was held communally and collectively.

I first met Chief Deng Majok Kuol Arop and Chief Deng Makuei (Deng Abot) Kuol Arop at one of these annual spiritual offerings at our home in Molbang when I was a child, before I went to school. The notion that I would overturn such a long tradition and work against the interest of the Ngok people of Abyei is preposterous. This is a very long affinity which the young politicians of Abyei are abusing, and I fear it could cause long-term damage to the cause of the Ngok people of Abyei.

This book covers not only the facts of the Abyei political situation as I know them, but also the historical relationships between the communities that I have had the privilege to know and to work with, socially and politically, at various levels of political representation in Sudan, before and after the South split from the North.

Traditionally, before the Arop Biong, or the Kuol Arop Biong family, decided to join the political administration of Northern Sudan under British colonial rule, the two sections, Ngok Kuol Arop and Kuac Madut Ring, were a close cultural community. This was before any serious colonial administration could take root. It was assumed that the two sections were one: they always had a close affinity, acting together on any issue of mutual concern. Clearly, Arop Biong had the final say; that is, until the question arose during British rule of joining the administration of Kordofan.

Arop Biong assumed that Kuac Anganya, or Kuac Madut Ring, would follow his decision to be part of Northern Sudan. The British colonial officials do not seem to have had a position on this. The whole future of South Sudan was unstable, especially as the Nilotic tribes of South Sudan, the Dinka and the Nuer, were still resisting British colonial rule. So when Kuac Madut Ring decided not to join the Ngok people of Abyei in being administered as part of Kordofan province of Northern Sudan, the British administrators of Bahr el Ghazal, still a sub-province of Equatoria, decided not to give Kuac six sections. Instead, they decided to attach Kuac to Akuar under Chief Juk Chom. One of the six sections of Kuac, called Anganya, under sub-chief Akueei Teeng, requested to be annexed to Amuol of Chief Bol Nyuol. The Amuol were maternal uncles to sub-chief Akueei Teeng, who was later succeeded by his son, Teeng Akueei, but remained at Amuol.

The five sub-chiefs of Kuac were now part of Akuar, under Chief Juk Chom, but against their will. This was before my father's time.

The five sub-chiefs of Kuac stayed together in Akuar and always acted together. They continued to aspire towards their own chiefdom, and put forward this demand whenever the opportunity arose.

When my father came of age and took over the sub-chiefdom of his Aher Kuac section, one of the five Kuac sub-chiefdoms, the demand for an independent Kuac chiefdom resurfaced in earnest. There was no public gathering of the Gogrial district authority when the five sub-chiefs of Kuac did not demand to have their own chiefdom (Baany Alama Thiith). My father, as the leader of Kuac, became known for this crusade to achieve Kuac chiefdom. The last British district commissioner of Gogrial, Ranald Boyle, used to refer to me as a rebel like my father, because of the political stand I took over the years for the cause of South Sudan; a much larger cause than a tribal chiefdom, of course.

In spite of the fact that my father had been appointed deputy chief of the entire Akuar and Kuac sections and deputy president of Akuar and Kuac chiefs' court, striving for the independence of Kuac never waned for him. Kuac, although a section of Akuar, never lost its independent identity and became known as Kuac Madut Ring. It was the SPLM movement that finally recognized the full chiefdom of Kuac Madut Ring and gave my father his last wish in life, only a short while before his death.

While my father was alive, although he was always very close to Chief Deng Majok Kuol Arop, he was concerned that the Ngok Dinka people of Abyei should remain part of Northern Sudan, even though Southern Sudan itself had now become part of a greater Sudan. My father often told me that he could not see a future for the Ngok people in Northern Sudan – he was a separatist through and through when it came to relations with Northern Sudan. To him, Northern Sudan was a distinct Arab and Islamic culture into which the Dinka could not fit. The Dinka never believed in being assimilated or in assimilating other peoples.

There was always something unusual about the attitude many of the Dinka chiefs held regarding their relationship with Northern Sudan. They did not think that it could last, or that it could be good. My father always told me that he wished the politics of South Sudan, with which I had become involved, could change the situation of 'Our Ngok people of Abyei'. I never lost sight of his strong desire to help Abyei.

Chief Giir Thiik Kero, one of the wisest, most prominent and industrious of Dinka chiefs, had become a close personal friend to me. Chief Giir Thiik knew my relationship with Chief Deng Majok Kuol Arop. Whenever I had the opportunity to have a chat with Chief Giir Thiik, and the Abyei issue cropped up in the conversation, he would say: 'Have you not persuaded your Uncle Deng Majok to return his people back home to the South?' While my answer was always 'Not yet', this was not always an honest answer.

Apart from on the occasions related in this book, I had not seriously attempted to persuade Deng Majok Kuol Arop to return with the Ngok people of Abyei to the South. This was because there was no South to persuade the Ngok people to return to. The South was always a bloody civil war arena. The lives of South Sudanese there were subject to liquidation with impunity at any time by the powers that be. It was no place to ask one's people to return to. But for noble traditional leaders such as Chief Giir Thiik Kero, it was always better to die amongst your people. That is why he wanted the Ngok people of Abyei to return to the South from the North in his lifetime.

When I visited Chief Giir Thiik in Juba in March 1973, where we had all gathered to mark the first anniversary of the 1972 Addis Ababa Peace Agreement with the North, he asked me why the chiefs were assembled. I told him that we were there to celebrate the peace agreement between the South and the North. He immediately asked, 'Is this the agreement of yesterday?' This was the Dinka metaphor for one year. When I answered him, 'Yes, it was this peace of yesterday', the Chief asked: 'Why do you not leave it to last ten years before you celebrate it?' Exactly ten years later to the day, the North abrogated the 1972 peace agreement and a civil war ensued that lasted more than twenty-one years. Unfortunately, Chief Giir Thiik Kero did not live long enough to see his words come true. The North had broken another peace agreement with the South. But I know for certain that the Chief and all our late parents would have been pleased to have witnessed an independent South Sudan, although they would also be distressed by the terrible damage and death that the rulers of South Sudan have inflicted on their people, because of material greed and hunger for power.

Chapter 1

How Abyei Became Part of
Northern Sudan

The story of the Ngok Dinka people of Abyei has become controversial, and the solution to their situation is daunting. Events in the territory are a classic example of how European colonialism made decisions that had no regard for the interests of the communities. Colonialism never consulted the local population, nor cared about the effects of its decisions on them. When the population was uneducated, as the Ngok Dinka were, the decisions of the colonial masters were regarded as laws and had to be respected as such. The tribal leaders did not have a say in decisions that affected the life and welfare of their communities. To keep their jobs as tribal chiefs, their only responsibility was to respect and to carry out colonial decisions as closely and as loyally as possible.

So when the British in Sudan decided in 1905 to annex the small Ngok Dinka territory of Abyei, so that it would be administered as part of Southern Kordofan, they did not consider how this decision would affect the life of the local community. The ethnic leaders had to accept that the Ngok Dinka of Abyei had become part of Kordofan province and, therefore, part of Northern Sudan. In the mind of the ordinary Dinka, Northern Sudan was an Arab land that had no affinity whatsoever to the Dinka; but the ordinary Dinka had no say in the matter.

Over time, the Messiria Baggara Arabs of Southern Kordofan attempted to incorporate the Ngok Dinka land that the British had annexed to them. They cared little about what the Ngok Dinka felt. The Arabs lacked a land with pasture and water, especially during the dry season of the year. They felt they had been given it on a silver platter.

The Ngok Dinka did not accept this encroachment into their land without their consent, nor did the larger population of the Ngok Dinka of Abyei consider themselves part of Kordofan, as it separated them from their kith and kin, the larger Dinka population to the south, in Bahr el Ghazal and Upper Nile.

An ineffective but vigorous political debate between the educated members of the Ngok Dinka community – the majority of whom were encouraged by the British to follow an education in the South Sudanese pattern (that is, in English rather than in Arabic) – led to political agitation for the return of Abyei to South Sudan. This opened up a schism between the educated and the traditional tribal leadership. Having accepted the colonial decision to annex them to the North, the ethnic leadership, the tribal chiefs, had to make do with what they had been given.

Unfortunately, because the Ngok Dinka community was so small (with one chiefdom alone), the ethnic leadership of the Ngok Dinka was dominated by just one family, the Arop Biong family. In the period we are studying the protagonists were Chief Arop Biong, his son, Kuol Arop Biong, and *his* son, Deng Majok Kuol Arop Biong; his sons, in turn, have taken over the chieftainship.

The family of Chief Arop Biong has had a better relationship with the Messiria Baggara Arabs than many of the Ngok Dinka of Abyei. This has led to educated members of the Ngok Dinka accusing them of having remained part of Southern Kordofan for purely personal and family interests. This accusation is not totally accurate, since there were always more important public interests for the powers in Abyei to safeguard and protect, not just for the Ngok Dinka of Abyei but, at the very least, the larger Dinka interest south of Abyei. As an example, the encroachment of the Messiria Baggara Arabs on Dinka land, especially during the dry season grazing period, had an impact beyond the Ngok Dinka territory. Accusations against rulers, whether political or administrative, are not always fair or accurate.

Quite conceivably, the Baggara Messiria Arabs could have defeated the Ngok Dinka and occupied their territory. Rather than let that happen, Arop Biong and his successors thought it was their duty to normalize relations in the interest of their subjects. This meant that messages of

Chief Deng Majok in the late 1950s, when he was in his late fifties. (From *The Man Called Deng Majok*, through the courtesy and generosity of the author, Francis Mading Deng Majok Kuol Arop)

friendliness were sent, if not always togetherness. Unfortunately this did not work, and hostilities between the two sides became the order of the day. The Ngok Dinka of Abyei found it hard to be part of Northern Sudan.

The challenging relationship between the Dinka as a whole (and not just the Ngok Dinka of Abyei) and the Messiria Baggara Arabs of Southern Kordofan was a constant. Responsible Dinka chiefs south of Abyei always appreciated this, and it should not be lost sight of in today's heated debate about the future of Abyei.

I recall the importance my father attached to the responsibilities shouldered by his contemporary, Chief Deng Majok Kuol Arop, in handling the Messiria Baggara Arabs' continuous encroachment on Dinka land. My father always referred to him as 'a chief to all the Dinka, because of the heavy responsibility he was handling on all our behalf'. The chief had earned for himself, both from Messiria Baggara Arab chiefs such as Chief Babo Nimir, and from Dinka chiefs such as my father, the right and the responsibility to settle disputes between the two tribes over the common borders between Southern Kordofan and Northern Bahr el Ghazal. This was at a time when the authority of the British colonial administration was waning, when the chief was the authority, as well as everything else. After independence, in the mid-1970s, when Nimeiri's military dictatorship abolished native administration in Northern Sudan without setting up a credible replacement, everything fell apart, and the social and administrative condition of the Ngok Dinka people of Abyei suddenly deteriorated.

After Sudan became independent from Britain, the political relationship between Northern Sudan and South Sudan deteriorated; indeed, the situation escalated into war and many educated young people from Abyei joined South Sudan's liberation struggle. This complicated the Ngok Dinka of Abyei's position. Because the politics of South Sudan and Northern Sudan remain complicated, even after South Sudan attained independence from Northern Sudan on 9 July 2011, it is still difficult, at the time of writing, to deduce what will happen to the Ngok Dinka of Abyei.

The Messiria Baggara Arabs now regard Abyei as part of their territory. Equally, the Ngok Dinka of Abyei regard themselves as part of South Sudan. The government of South Sudan and the government of Northern Sudan each regard Abyei as their territory. Instead of these two governments seeing themselves as catalysts that could help to resolve the Abyei conflict, they are involved in a political dispute. This, in itself, is the latest of the many mistakes that have been made.

Even the British colonial authority, which in 1905 annexed Abyei to Northern Sudan, came to the realization before this occurred that Abyei could not survive as a Dinka territory if its administration stayed in Kordofan. Because of this they attempted to reverse their 1905 decision and to restore Abyei, as a Dinka territory, to the South – to Bahr el Ghazal. Unfortunately, it was too late. Many interests had already become too entrenched, and the political elite of Northern Sudan lost patience with the British colonial administration.

I witnessed one of the last attempts by the British to reverse their decision. This was in March 1952, when they convened an inter-provincial conference in Abyei town, hoping that they could persuade Chief Deng Majok Kuol Arop and his community to return to South Sudan. It was a well-planned and well-prepared conference, lasting for five days, which was attended by the governors of Kordofan and Darfur, both from Northern Sudan, and the governors of Bahr el Ghazal and Upper Nile from South Sudan, together with all their neighbouring district commissioners. The Dinka chiefs of Bahr el Ghazal and Upper Nile were also invited, and this included my father. I was very privileged because my father decided to take me along with him, even though I was still young: I had just completed my second year at Comboni Fathers Catholic school at Bussere, just a few miles south of Wau town.

Although my father had decided I should carry on with my education, his underlying plan was always that I would one day replace him as the chief of Kuac Angany, better known as Kuac Madut Ring – hence his desire for me to accompany him to such an important meeting. He had always emphasized to me that the Ngok Dinka people of Abyei, as well as being our close neighbours, were part of our family.

A huge camp had been prepared to house the Dinka chiefs who had been invited to the Abyei Conference, but Chief Deng Majok Kuol Arop decided that my father, his wife and I should stay with him in his own house. This was a special treat for me, because two of the chief's

sons, Francis Mading Deng Kuol and Zacharia Bol Deng Kuol, who
were my contemporaries, were staying in the same compound. During
my stay, the only time I parted company with Francis and Zacharia
was when I attended the conference sessions: I did not miss a single
one. Francis and Zacharia, in contrast, chose to stay away from the
conference entirely. We never discussed why they made that decision.
It did not occur to me at the time that it was important to understand
the reasons, but, in retrospect, given how interested and involved they
have become as adults in resolving their people's problems, it would be
interesting to understand their thinking.

For five long days I sat on the floor of the conference shed, literally
under my father's chair. Those were the good old days. Security at such
huge gatherings was never an issue. No one bothered to ask why such
a young lad was in attendance. It was a moving experience, one that I
still remember vividly to this day, sixty years later.

The British colonial governor of Bahr el Ghazal, Richard Owen,
the man to whose province the Ngok Dinka would have returned, was
very active at the conference, giving Chief Deng Majok Kuol Arop
all the possible guarantees he could possibly require if he decided to
return to Bahr el Ghazal. In addition, all the Dinka chiefs spoke with
persuasive eloquence.

One of the most impressive and most fiery interventions was made
by Chief Deng Majok Kuol's uncle, Mahdi Arop Biong. Not a chief
himself and therefore not invited to the conference, Elderman Mahdi
Arop, who was a spearman, a Dinka spiritual leader, decided he had
to express his own views. Adorned in his traditional long red robe and
carrying all his spiritual spears, he marched alone towards the conference shed. When Chief Deng Majok Kuol noticed him, he ordered
his local retainers – policemen – to prevent the old elderman from
approaching the conference, and to forcefully lead him away.

However, Elderman Mahdi Arop began shouting at the top of
his voice. 'I want the conference to hear my opinion. What kind of a
meeting discusses the future of the people but does not want to hear
the opinion of the people?' His shouting was audible in the conference,
and Governor Richard Owen ordered his own police guards to bring
Mahdi Arop to him. The elderman was stripped of his spiritual spears

and guided to the centre of the conference, where Richard Owen asked him to speak. A humorous Dinka orator, Elderman Mahdi Arop turned to Chief Deng Majok Kuol, who had been murmuring to the conference that his uncle was a madman, and addressed him directly. 'My dear nephew, this is heaven intervening on behalf of the Ngok Dinka people of Abyei. Only God has inspired all these people to come here. Do not confuse your word to them, my dear nephew.' The chief heckled his uncle throughout, but Elderman Mahdi Arop paid no attention and continued to address the conference.

Turning to the Dinka chiefs from Bahr el Ghazal, all seated in a semi-circle at the centre of the conference, he said: 'One of the reasons why the senior British colonial officials organized this conference to return the Ngok Dinka to their roots is because we have not fitted with the North Sudan Arabs culturally. When grown-up people are seated as you Dinka chiefs now are, in this conference, the Dinka do not call elders by their given name. They address them by their bull name as a sign of respect and of dignity. Let me now address you by your bull names.' He began with Chief Giir Thiik Kero, addressing him as 'Giir Mangar', addressed Chief Bol Chol as 'Bol Turjok' and so on, through a long list. The nearest neighbours to the Ngok Dinka of Abyei, my father, was the last one whom Elderman Mahdi Arop named – 'Madut Dhongchol'.

Mahdi Arop then turned to the Messiria Baggara Arab chiefs, and said to his nephew: 'You see, these are all elderly and respectable people. But the Arabs do not call themselves by their bull names. No matter how elderly and respectable they are, the Arab chiefs are still called by their first names, like children. Now, let me ask you, my nephew, to address the Arab chiefs. Are you not going to call Babo Nimir by his first name of Babo, as if he was still a child?'

The elderman finally pleaded with Chief Deng Majok Kuol not to miss the golden opportunity that was being given to return the Ngok people to the South, yet in spite of all his pleas, and those of all the Dinka chiefs from Bahr el Ghazal and Upper Nile, the chief remained adamant that he would stay put in Kordofan, Northern Sudan.

Governor Richard Owen of Bahr el Ghazal would not give up. He invited Chief Deng Majok Kuol and his sub-chiefs and eldermen

Chief Deng Majok (foreground, fourth from left) with Arab chiefs in an intertribal celebration, 1954. (From *The Man Called Deng Majok*, through the courtesy and generosity of the author, Francis Mading Deng Majok Kuol Arop)

to tour the six Dinka districts of Bahr el Ghazal, Gogrial, Aweil, Tonj, Rumbek, Yirol and Wau, to acquaint himself with how the Dinka native administration was organized. When the tour was completed, however, the chief stuck firm with his decision to remain in the North.

Many anecdotes followed the chief's tour of Bahr el Ghazal. There were comments about how poor the Dinka chiefs of the South were compared with the chiefs of Northern Sudan. As part of their plan to keep the South Sudanese tribal chiefs 'native', the British colonial authorities had decided not to equalize the salary scale for chiefs and government officials between the South and the North, thereby not improving their economic lot lest they lost touch with their primitive nature.

Chief Deng Majok Kuol Arop's salary in Northern Sudan at this time was Ls. 40 (40 Sudanese pounds per month). My father's salary, which I had the privilege as his son to receive and to spend on my school needs, was only Ls. 3 (3 Egyptian pounds) per month.

(The exchange rate at the time between the British and the Egyptian pound, the currency then in circulation in Sudan, was one to one.) The national government of Sudan doubled South Sudanese chiefs' salaries after independence, and in return expected absolute loyalty to the government in Khartoum. Yet salaries in Northern Sudan remained many times higher than in the South, which fuelled resentment in the South against the North.

There were also important internal reasons why the leaders and elders of the Ngok Dinka community of Abyei wanted to be part of Northern Sudan. First, the Ngok chiefs, headed by the Kuol Arop family, decided the only way they could prevent perpetual tribal warfare with the Messiria Baggara Arabs was to belong together in the same region and administration. In this way, the Arabs would regard Ngok Dinka as part of their community, while the Dinka chiefs' decree that the common border north of the River Kiir should be peaceful would be merely an administrative order for the Arabs and the Ngok Dinka chiefs alike. It was traditionally well known and accepted that the Baggara would not obey the decree in full – they never obeyed any orders to the letter – but at least they would know that these rules were being laid down by their own chiefs, and that if there was punishment for disobedience it would be their chiefs who imposed it.

Chief Deng Majok Kuol Arop, in particular, became a towering leader in his own right. His word was tantamount to law amongst his people , and no one could disobey his orders with impunity. This helped to keep the peace with all his neighbours, not just the Baggara Messiria Arabs but also the Twic Dinka, south of Abyei.

For many of these cattle-rearing tribes, grazing was a very well-organized affair. A system was established whereby the chiefs from Southern Kordofan, who included Chief Deng Majok Kuol Arop and the Twic Mayardit Dinka chiefs, and the Baggara Arab chiefs met every October either in Abyei or in Turalei, the Twic Dinka court centre. This meeting demarcated the areas along the River Kiir where the Baggara Arabs could graze and water their livestock during the dry season. The chiefs normally appointed representatives to monitor the grazing and watering patterns. The Arabs were not allowed to cross the river with their cattle to the grazing territory of the Dinka, and vice versa. These simple rules were largely obeyed by the two ethnic communities, because the chiefs were in charge of the administration of their own people and were respected. The chiefs knew who the troublemakers were in their communities, and kept a vigilant eye on these trouble makers.

The law-abiding nature of the tribes can be illustrated by the following anecdote. Sometimes, when the rainy season had been poor and the pasture along the River Kiir (Bahr el Arab) had suffered, the Baggara Arabs asked permission to cross into Dinka territory south of the Dinka permanent settlement, known as *toch*, which straddles the banks of another river, the Lol, which is entirely in the Dinka country. More often than not, that permission was obtained from my father, because his area lay directly south of the border to the north with the Ngok Dinka of Abyei. The Arabs were never allowed to cross the River Lol, because south of the Lol was the boundary between the Dinka and the Nuer. Nor were the Arabs permitted to cross into Akocyic, a lush dry season grazing land, full of valuable wild foods and fish, where only the Dinka were allowed to graze. This was my father's territory, and he only allowed other Dinka cattle camps, even from Aweil-Abiem, to graze and water there.

An incident occurred in 1952 or 1953, at the end of the Messiria Baggara Arab grazing season. The Arabs had been allowed to graze at Lolkou and were returning to Kordofan with their herd. They decided to capture and take along with them a large number of Dinka cattle, just over 100 head. Rather than cause a security incident, the cattle owners reported the theft to my father. It was the school vacation season and I was still at home. The Dinka told him it was Awallat Kamil, one of the Messiria Arab ethnic groups, which was responsible for the theft. Chief Babo Nimir, the Messiria Arab paramount chief, was at the Baggara Arab camp, not far from our home, when my father heard the news. He had come to the area to instruct the Messiria herders to return home, because rains were threatening.

Chief Babo Nimir and my father were old acquaintances. My father asked me to accompany him to the chief's cattle camp, so he could inform the chief of what his people had done. Naturally, I was delighted to be allowed to witness such an important encounter, and to see how the Messiria Arabs and Dinka chiefs settled problems between their groups. As we approached the Arab camp, Chief Babo Nimir sent one of his retainers to meet us and take us to him.

My father had a crowd of Dinka young men accompanying him. They stood back as soon as they recognized Babo Nimir's people. When Babo Nimir stood up to greet my father, he knew at once that there was something wrong, yet, all the same, he greeted my father very warmly.

My father introduced me to Chief Babo Nimir, saying that I was his eldest son and at school. Chief Babo Nimir was pleased at this, and asked if my father had other children at school. My father said I was the only one.

Tea was served, and then my father related to Chief Babo Nimir that Awallat Kamil had taken a sizeable herd of Dinka cattle. The chief asked my father several times if he was sure it was Awallat Kamil. My father was definite. He then asked my father to return to his home and said he would look into the matter; that if the Dinka cattle were taken by Awallat Kamil, my father should rest assured that he would get back his people's cattle.

The following morning, as my father and some of his elders were taking tea, the entire herd of Dinka cattle was returned. My father asked the owners to check and report back to him – and not a single cow was missing. The matter had been amicably resolved, and the Messiria Baggara Arabs returned to Kordofan at the end of another successful dry season in Dinka country.

Much later, I came to know Chief Babo Nimir personally, even calling him 'Uncle'. I met him frequently when I became a member of the Sudanese parliament, first elected in 1968, and as minister of culture and information under President Jaafar Mohamed Nimeiri, between 1972 and 1979.

I had the privilege to remind Uncle Babo Nimir of this story about the cattle taken by Awallat Kamal, and remarked upon how he knew who had taken the cattle and managed to return them so quickly. He took a very special pride in explaining to me how things worked in those days: 'You cannot be a successful chief if you do not know your people well. You have to know who is a criminal and a thief amongst your people,' he said. 'When your father told me that the Dinka cattle had been taken by Awallat Kamil, I knew immediately who these Awallat Kamil were. After you and your father left our camp, I immediately asked these thieves to be brought to me. I did not ask them whether or not they had taken the Dinka cattle. I simply told them that I wanted all the Dinka cattle at my camp that night. All the cattle were collected and returned to my camp that same night. Because it was already dark, I could only return the Dinka cattle to your father the next day.' Chief Babo Nimir then went on to compliment my father for accurately identifying the Arabs who took the Dinka cattle. 'What your father did is the right duty of a good chief – you see.'

Both Chief Babo Nimir and myself served in at least two public investigation commissions set up by President Jaafar Nimeiri. While I was minister under Nimeiri, there were many matters of common interest concerning which the chief sought my help, and I had the honour and privilege of resolving them.

One of the worst decisions of the Nimeiri regime was the abolition of the native administration in Northern Sudan. During the early years of the Nimeiri regime, between May 1969 – when Nimeiri took power in a military coup – and 1971, the Communist Party of Sudan held great sway over the government. When the regime decreed the abolition of native administration in Northern Sudan, overnight there were no chiefs, no police and no judges. The huge tribal administrative set-up, so well organized by the British colonial administration and which had kept law and order on the cheap, was dissolved without a replacement. Survival of the fittest became the order of the day. Even South Sudan, whose native administration had not been dissolved, was badly affected, partly because civil war was already raging there and partly because the dissolution of the native administration disrupted many activities along the border.

The leaders of the Communist Party of Sudan would argue that they had an alternative to the native administration in the North, but the return to power of Jaafar Mohamed Nimeiri only three days after the communist coup in November 1971 put paid to it. But who in Sudan, South and North, can excuse the Communist Party of Sudan for biting off more than they could chew – first by filling the Nimeiri regime with their members during the initial stages of Nimeiri's successful coup on 25 May 1969 and then by toppling Nimeiri himself in November 1971, when they could not guarantee that this would be successful. What it all added up to, in my opinion, was that the leaders of the Sudan Communist Party were a bunch of reckless adventurers who took steps that cost them their own lives, and the country so much. It is unfortunate that the same pattern seems to be unfolding in South Sudan today. Bad history repeats itself, whether in the North or the South.

As political tensions grew between the South and Northern Sudan, and the political elite in the South began to weigh up their options, the position of the Dinka people of Abyei became increasingly untenable. As South Sudan's political elite began to make demands, starting with the August 1955 uprising in Torit, Eastern Equatoria, by the South Sudanese contingent of the Sudan Defence Force, politics between Northern Sudan and South Sudan took on a racial and religious configuration. The Northern elite decided that they would not share power with the South, nor would they let the South take a political stand that could result in a break-up of the country. Any political utterance that smacked of equality with the North, let alone separation of the South from the North, had to be suppressed. This suppression extended to the educated sons of the Ngok Dinka of Abyei, most of whom, as we have seen, had been educated in line with the South Sudan educational pattern, which was non-Arab and non-Islamic.

When the first prime minister of Sudan, Ismail el Azhari, decided that what had begun to happen in the South since August 1955 was merely a storm in a tea cup, and that he would proceed with his pan-Arab/pan-Islamic agenda for Sudan, without first addressing the political grievances of the South, any proposal for the unity of Sudan which a tiny territorial enclave such as Abyei may have thought they could put forward was doomed. Abyei was now in a no-win situation. It could not decide to become part of South Sudan, because that was no longer within its role or power. Having refused to accept British colonial advice to return to the South in 1952, just four years before the British were due to leave the country at independence, Abyei was now a Northern Sudanese territory. This may not have mattered that much if Northern Sudan had accommodated views that were not its own – that is, views that were neither Arabic nor Islamic, like those views about Abyei. The Ngok Dinka elite had clearly thrown in its lot with the South, for what it was worth. But after August 1955, South Sudan was a country to be repressed into submission. How could Abyei survive this situation while geographically remaining part of the North?

The Messiria Baggara Arabs saw their window of opportunity, and absorbed the Ngok Dinka territory into their own; this included Abyei, the territory, not just the town. They say that it is through their kindness and generosity they have invited the Ngok Dinka to settle in Abyei.

This claim has been reinforced by the Ngok leaders of the SPLM, who state that Abyei can only settle its cause with the North through a military stand-off between the two states, North and South. This ignores the possibility of political resolution of the conflict between the two indigenous people of Southern Kordofan. In failing to accept that this is a local dispute, and fostering the false contention that the Abyei conflict is between Khartoum and Juba, means that the real mediators are denied a role in bringing about resolution of this rather intricate issue.

Abyei is not a dispute between Khartoum and Juba. All that they need to do in order to cooperate is to implement the Abyei protocol of the CPA, so that the Ngok Dinka people of Abyei can decide on their future. Both Juba and Khartoum are bound by the terms of the protocol. No section of the CPA has an expiry date, and all sections of this important international treaty must be addressed, however long this takes.

One of the tragedies of the land called Sudan is that no one wants to sit down with the other side to explain a point and to prove it peacefully. With the educated Ngok Dinka elite now intrinsically part of a struggling South Sudan, the Abyei situation has been put on a war footing and is very difficult for the political movement of South Sudan to handle, or even to explain to the Ngok Dinka people.

It is not easy to completely arrive at the facts relating to any historical and political story in any part of colonial Africa. For one, the native communities have historically not been interested in events beyond their own locality, and the facts pertaining to their own area

were conveyed orally. But security, particularly internal security that
had immediate ramifications, concerned them very deeply, and they
needed to interest themselves in the affairs of their neighbours but
without interfering. Those who did interfere considered themselves
more powerful, and were able to occupy their weaker neighbours' land
by force and get away with it. But in general 'live and let live' was a
principle that seemed to suit much of the traditional way of life for
native Africans.

Having said that, this was not always the case amongst the South
Sudanese communities in respect of the immigrant Arab tribes from
Northern Sudan. These tribes mostly travelled from the Arabian Gulf
region, coming in search of many things that were plentifully available in Sudan – land, water, pasture and, most controversially, slaves.
With better weaponry and tight organization, the Arabs conquered
much of Northern Sudan from the current Nilotic communities of the
Republic of South Sudan. At the time, what one captured remained
one's own. And it is an accepted natural law that if a community
captured territory and lived in it for a certain length of time, that land
belonged to it.

Therefore, it seems likely that the Nilotic communities of South
Sudan – the Shuluk, the Nuer and the Dinka – are traceable to Northern
Sudan and along the River Nile. Whether or not this is the case, clearly
the Nilotic communities now occupy land that they call their own,
but must have belonged to other communities before them, who were
weaker than them and whom they had to force out.

This brief explanation underscores how the Ngok Dinka of Abyei
became part of Northern Sudan. The young revolutionary leaders in
South Sudan today find it easy to accuse their people of being uneducated in the past, and therefore not enlightened enough to look after
the interests of their communities. Sometimes they even accuse traditional leaders of the recent past of being motivated by personal gain.
However, a critical examination of the history of a small territory
such as Abyei indicates that these ethnic community leaderships were
always very carefully selected, even before some semblance of government came into being. Native communities in general had their own
way of selecting leadership. Qualifications were rigorous. As a primary

consideration, the leader had to be a man of his word. His word had to be spiritual; what he told the community had to sound spiritually acceptable to God. The Dinka always believed in God. Since God was not always visible, he was represented on earth by some symbol that the community related to, that symbol being associated with some past goodness that had occurred.

The outsiders, the colonial powers, who came from Europe to invade and exploit Africa, not only to plunder but also to convert Africa to Christianity, belittled and disparaged native spiritual beliefs. The same was the case with the Arab invaders in respect to Islam. Only written religions were to be accepted in colonial Africa; so Christianity and Islam predominate in the continent today. But for the natives, who had no contact with either Christianity or Islam, the traditional symbols of their beliefs held sway. It was therefore very important in the tribal tradition of leadership selection amongst the Dinka, and indeed amongst all the other ethnic groups, that certain qualifications had to be available in the leader:

First, he or she (the Dinka had women leaders in many of their communities) had to be a truthful individual.

Second, the leader had to be an individual who was well to do: the Dinka believe that only those who possess wealth of their own will not be tempted to enrich themselves with public wealth.

Third, the leader of the community had to be someone whose word was spiritually inspired: the leader should be God-fearing. Only then would his or her rule and word of direction become acceptable to God and be God-endowed.

Finally, the leader had to be an individual of strong personal courage; he or she should not be afraid of speaking the truth to anyone under their command, no matter how strong, powerful and wealthy that individual might be. Unfortunately, all these qualifications and qualities have become so eroded that the opposite qualities appear to be the new qualifications for political, administrative, community, spiritual and government leadership.

When Arop Biong first decided that he wanted his people to be part of Northern Sudan and to be administered together with the Messiria Baggara Arabs, his only consideration was how to prevent disputes between the Ngok Dinka of Abyei and the Arabs. The Baggara Arabs were well known for being an unruly community by nature. If disputes arose over grazing areas or water, they did not agree to settle the issue at a Dinka court that they were not part of. Arop Biong had this in mind: these communities had no legal, political or even administrative recourse, and there was little government to speak of. Only the word of the powerful ruled the day.

Even the British colonial administration initially had to acquiesce in what they found in Sudan. When colonial authority was extended there, it did so rather gradually. Colonialism first had to establish itself in the main centres of Northern Sudan, such as Khartoum, but was unable to spread out to the countryside, as there were no police, no judges or courts, no rule of law. The rural hinterland had to rely on its own systems. The British, therefore, had to endorse and sanction what they found to be working on the ground – that is, community leadership or, in their own terminology, native administration.

Being in one province, under one district administration and one native administrative court, the Baggara Arabs recognized that they were one people with the Ngok Dinka of Abyei. This did not mean that enduring problems were automatically resolved. Many still remained, but since these problems came to one and the same court and the chiefs who had to handle them recognized that they belonged together, the problems were manageable.

Even those problems that arose between the neighbouring Dinka communities south of Abyei – in Bahr el Ghazal and Upper Nile – with the Baggara Arabs were controllable, because of the Ngok Dinka chief of Abyei, whether this was Deng Majok Kuol Arop or his father Kuol Arop Biong or his grandfather Arop Biong. It was easy for any of the Ngok chiefs to set up court to resolve disputes between the Baggara Arabs and any of the Dinka sections, even those south of Abyei. The Dinka communities of the South in both Bahr el Ghazal and Upper Nile – the Twic Mayardit of Gogrial, the Malual Giernyang of Aweil and the Rueng and Panaru of Bentiu – always looked to the Ngok Dinka chief of Abyei for help whenever there was a problem between any of them and the Messiria Baggara Arabs. Both sides looked to the Ngok chief as someone who would be fair to them in the resolution of any conflict.

Because of the role of the Ngok chiefs, and because of the modus oper-
andi that evolved between the traditional leadership on both sides, it
was always easy and simple to resolve matters between the Baggara
Arabs and the Dinka through the help of the Ngok Dinka chief.

I came to know and admire three other Northern Sudanese community chiefs besides Chief Babo Nimir of the Messiria Baggara Arabs,
and I want to mention them here. The first of them was Chief Surur
Mohamed Romili of Khartoum. He was a member with me in the border
commission set up by President Nimeiri. Both he and Babo Nimir knew
what tampering with ethnic borders between communities can do, not
only to bordering ethnic communities but to the whole country. Their
stand that no one should tamper with traditional borders made it easy
for our border commission to recommend to President Jaafar Mohamed
Nimeiri not to tamper with the existing colonial provincial borders
between the South and the North.

Although President Nimeiri was not happy with our commission
report, because he was very much behind the idea of redrawing the
borders in order to put the oil wells at Unity, South Sudan, in the North,
he had to accept the report. He dissolved our commission without
publishing its recommendations, but also did not implement the border
demarcations recommended by his new ministry of internal affairs, on
the advice of his new Attorney General, Hassan Abdalla el Turabi.

President Nimeiri was by now under the strong influence of his
new-found allies in the National Islamic Front, led by Hassan Abdalla
al-Turabi, and the team that he had brought into Nimeiri's regime,
including Sharif el Tuhami, the minister of energy. Nimeiri had ordered
that the borders between the South and the North be redrawn, with the
intention of cutting the areas of Western Nuer of Upper Nile from the
South and annexing them to the North. Al-Turabi in effect influenced
Nimeiri to rename what was known in the traditional colonial maps
as the Western Nuer district of Upper Nile as Unity province, with its
headquarters at Bentin, this district being where the US oil company
Chevron had just discovered oil. In the end, Chevron had to place its
operational headquarters at Muglad, in Kordofan, where no oil had
been found at the time of this writing.

As the debate over the oil find in South Sudan raged on and the bias against the South – where the discovery of oil was well established – showed its head, Chevron, which had discovered the oil in the South, became heavily influenced by Khartoum and the new ministry of energy. Finally, Chevron's country director, Bell Bellenger, threatened to withdraw the company from Sudan unless they were allowed to deal with the central government in Khartoum without any interference from the South. This was, of course, just one of the many threats that were deployed against the South at that time. Had the friends of Khartoum inside Chevron really thought well about it, they would have realized that closing down oil operations in the South was actually what the South's representatives would have welcomed, as this would have been better than letting Khartoum add oil revenue from the South to the resources it could draw upon in order to continue to repress the South. Naturally, as the war raged on in the South, and with Chevron having made Muglad its operational headquarters for South Sudan, the increasingly active guerrilla army of South Sudan, the SPLA, attacked and closed South Sudan's oil operation.

By the time the current ruling regime in Khartoum seized power in a military coup on 30 June 1989, and invited Chevron back to Sudan, other political issues had intervened and the new regime in Khartoum had become an outlaw regime as far as the United States was concerned, regarded in Washington as a sponsor of international terrorism because of its Islamic agenda. It thus became a power with which no US company could do business. The Islamic regime invited in alternative companies to produce the country's oil, and fuelled the debate between the South and the North about resource sharing.

Facts about the location and ownership of oil have been so distorted that it is difficult to properly discern the truth. And this distortion is not, unfortunately, confined to Northern Sudan and the political leadership of the North alone. Looking at the larger picture, if a credible solution to the current Abyei situation is not easy to achieve, it is because some of those who now regard themselves as the solution to the Abyei cause have not been honest with themselves, with their communities or with the international community. Falsehood has, regrettably, become such a powerful tool in the politics of South Sudan that many who want to speak the truth always need to think of their own personal and family security before speaking out.

Another prominent Northern Sudanese tribal chief whom I came to know well and to whom I became close was Mohamed Ahmed Abu Sin, the chief of the Shukria Arab ethnic group of the Gezira, in the Blue Nile region of Northern Sudan. Abu Sin was Sudan's first minister of information at the time of independence in January 1956.

When I became minister of culture and information in the government of President Jaafar Mohamed Nimeiri, after July 1972, when Nimeiri ended the civil war in South Sudan – by signing the March 1972 Addis Ababa Peace Agreement with the South and granting South Sudan self-government – there were only two former Northern Sudanese ministers of information still alive and active in Sudan. Mohamed Ahmed Abu Sin was the first Minister of Information in Sudan in 1954, when Sudan set up its first self-government before independence. He was already a popular and renowned Sudanese leader in his own right. Since the interim arrangements for the independence of Sudan were the responsibility of the British colonial authority, the new Sudanese political and constitutional system adopted the Westminster type of parliamentary organization.

When I became minister I adopted a policy of inviting any living former minister of information in Sudan to sit with me and to recollect their past experiences in the ministry. These invitations were individual and personal, and took place in private at my official residence, being issued six months after I had studied the conditions in the ministry of which I was now the head. I was preparing to write my policy document for discussion and approval by the council of ministers. Some of my public positions on national policies decided by the council of ministers had become public knowledge, and were openly being considered by ordinary citizens as courageous and positive for an individual who was serving under a military regime.

In spite of some good national policies, such as the peace agreement with the South, the Nimeiri regime was already considered by the public to be a dictatorship. I accepted a position in the regime extremely reluctantly, purely because it had just signed a peace agreement with the South and had granted regional autonomy – some form of small independence. My friends and colleagues who were running South Sudan from Juba wanted me to be part of the system that had given the South regional autonomy, thereby ending the seventeen year civil war.

Abel Alier Wal Kwai, whom Jaafar Mohamed Nimeiri had by now entrusted with running the affairs of the government of South Sudan on his behalf, had just been promoted to vice-president of the Republic, successfully leading the new government of Sudan delegation to the successful peace talks in Addis Ababa, Ethiopia, in March 1972. A personal friend and long-time political associate, Abel Alier wrote to me in November 1971, while I was preparing for my master's degree in journalism and international relations at Columbia University in New York – although I was to play no direct political role in the negotiations that finally led to the Addis Ababa peace agreement. Alier asked me in that letter to help intercede with two colleagues and contemporaries, Enoch Mading de Garang and Lawrence Wol Wol, who were leaders of the Anya-Nya liberation movement of South Sudan, and had been entrusted by the movement to negotiate with the government of Sudan.

In his letter, Abel Alier told me that Mading de Garang and Lawrence Wol Wol were not only the real brains and leaders of the Anya-Nya movement, but were also its principal negotiators. Alier wanted me to travel to London to talk to these two gentlemen, whom he described as rather intransigent. It was obvious to any serious-thinking South Sudanese that the best the South could hope for was a peace agreement with Khartoum that would grant some element of self-rule to the South that could be used as a basis for future negotiations.

I accepted Abel Alier's pleading. Having orchestrated the right of the South to self-determination at the 1965 Round Table Conference in Khartoum, we both clearly saw that the Nimeiri regime was weak enough to concede autonomy to the South at the Addis Ababa peace talks. But the regime was not so weak as to concede independence to the South; not yet, anyway.

Of course, Lawrence Wol Wol and Mading de Garang were privy to the fact that their movement was already receiving some military support from the state of Israel, and they did not want to jeopardize that support by seriously negotiating peace with Khartoum. But even if Israel was ready and willing to put up all the resources necessary for

South Sudan to win an outright military victory against Khartoum, there were other obstacles to overcome.

For one, the OAU had resolved that no colonial borders of Africa could be altered for any reason; that all countries had to respect the borders as they had been demarcated by the European colonial powers in Berlin in 1775. Each African country had the right to become independent from its colonial master, but not to change its borders. This policy made a mockery of nationalities, and the result is that African communities are terribly dislocated. Because of this policy, for example, the state of Biafra, which had successfully broken away from Nigeria in May 1967, was forced through war (1967–70) into being part of Nigeria once again.

In the case of South Sudan, one finds that national groups are split between neighbouring states, so ethnic communities are divided between two or more neighbours. For example, one finds the Nuer and the Anyuak in both South Sudan and Ethiopia; while the Acholi, the Madi, the Kuku, the Kakwa and others are shared between South Sudan and Uganda. The Zande of Western Equatoria of South Sudan are split between South Sudan, the Democratic Republic of Congo and the Central African Republic. No country can claim that they have more of a given ethnic community than their neighbours, because the numbers shift back and forth depending on which of the neighbours is more peaceful. Unpredictable and unstable movements make it difficult to demarcate borders accurately.

This is one of the main reasons why resolving the Abyei situation remains difficult. It is also why the Messiria Arabs, a people whose presence in Abyei has always been seasonal, now claim that Abyei belongs to them. It is a way of trying to hold on to a territory that is essential for their survival.

By the time I began my conversations with Sheikh Mohamed Ahmed Abu Sin, the former Minister of Information of Sudan, the Nimeiri regime had been in power for three years and its mistakes were the subject of conversations throughout the country and an object of ridicule by the public. I asked him why, as one of the prominent leaders and elders of Sudan, he did not join up with three or four others – such as Babo Nimir and Surur Romili – and go to Nimeiri to advise him about how to handle the affairs of state effectively. Sheikh Abu Sin replied that he had heard that when a courageous minister in the government of Nimeiri, such as Bona Malwal, told Nimeiri in the meeting of the Council of Ministers that he was wrong on any topic, Nimeiri would just fold his papers and walk away. The council meeting would end there and then. Sheikh Abu Sin then said that if the elders of Sudan spoke to Nimeiri and he did not like their advice, he would abruptly stop the meeting and walk away: 'We would all die there and then.' He realized that well-respected traditional leaders could not subject themselves to the indignity that they might encounter – even if, without transparency between any regime and its community, there is always a public exaggeration about what actually goes on.

Chief Surur Romili of Khartoum North, one of the three cities that make up the Sudanese capital, was also highly intelligent and very experienced. He was a member of Nimeiri's border commission with me. Neither Babo Nimir nor Surur Romili could understand why President Nimeiri had decided to set up a commission to redraw the borders between the South and the North. For them, Sudan was one country, with no possibility of being broken up. So why tamper with the existing borders? The attitude of these two Northern Sudanese chiefs from Southern Kordofan and from Khartoum North helped to form the final report of our border commission, which recommended to the president that he should not interfere with the current borders.

On one occasion Chief Surur Romili told the border commission, before the presence of the chief justice of Sudan, our chairman, how law and order had broken down in the country. This was in a conversation before formal discussions began. In Khartoum North, a judge was influenced by a lawyer friend of his, a lawyer for a wealthy merchant who owed a small amount of money to a poor Arab milkman. The milkman had been providing the merchant with a daily supply of milk, and over time the amount owed reached more than 300 Sudanese pounds, about 100 US dollars at that time. This was a relatively small sum for the merchant, but not for the milkman.

When the Arab milkman brought a case in the local court, the merchant hired a lawyer in order to deny the poor nomad his money. Unfortunately for the Arab, the judge was a colleague and friend of the lawyer. But the only thing they could do to deny the Arab nomad justice was to request a postponement of the case for three months every time it came before the court. Chief Surur Romili related to me that eventually the Arab merchant turned up in court. But the poor Arab nomad, not expecting any justice from the Sudanese court system, decided to take matters into his own hands. He was broke and had nothing to lose.

When the judge called the court session to order and asked the merchant's lawyer to speak, he recited the same old ritual; he wanted an adjournment for another three months. The judge picked up his court diary to make a note of this, and to mark the date of the next session. The poor Arab nomad pleaded with the judge to give him a second to speak. The judge was taken aback: how dare this nomad ask to speak when he had already ruled for adjournment? He turned to the Arab disdainfully, and said in a harsh tone, 'What do you want to say?'

The nomad had entered the court with a sharp knife at his elbow. He simply drew it without a word and struck the Arab merchant three times in the chest. The merchant fell down dead. The nomad then turned to the judge, told him he could postpone the case for as long as he wanted, then gave himself up to the court police.

Chief Surur Romili said to me that there was absolutely no rule of law in Sudan 'under your regime', turning to me as he said these last words: I was, of course, a cabinet minister of the regime before becoming a member of the border commission.

The last former minister of information whom I invited to my home was Abdel Mageed Abu Hassabu. Like me, he had been both a career journalist and a political activist. He was a lifetime member of the National Unionist Party of Ismail el Azhari (the founding prime minister of Sudan). It was Prime Minister el Azhari who appointed him as minister of information in the mid-1950s.

My meeting with Abdel Mageed Abu Hassabu over lunch took an entirely professional turn. The law to regulate media was vested in the minister of information, and he wanted to know what I would censor and why. When he left my home after several hours of conversation, I felt he was a very satisfied man, because I had assured him I would not engage in any censorship of anything. That would have been against my ethics as a professionally trained journalist. I also told him that if I ever engaged in media censorship of any kind, being a South Sudanese journalist with an interest in professional media that would be critical of the government of the day, I would suffer much more than any Northern Sudanese media that I would censor. We came to know each other well after this meeting, and I also know two of his children, a son and a daughter, both of whom followed their father into journalism and became my friends.

We should return to the core subject of this book, the cause of the Ngok Dinka people of Abyei. It is clear that the leaders of the educated Ngok Dinka of Abyei, who think that the only way forward for the people of Abyei is to return to South Sudan at all costs, consider the decision of their ancestors to take the Ngok people to the North to have been a mistake.

I have already mentioned in this chapter that no one has accurately recorded when Abyei became part of Kordofan, Northern Sudan. The date generally agreed is about 1905. This appears to have been the time when Arop Biong, the first traditional chief of the Ngok Dinka people of Abyei, was recorded as having chosen to be administered as part of Kordofan. Because the British colonial administration of Northern Sudan was still tenuous and the colonial administration of South Sudan non-existent, colonialism had to content itself with the vestiges of administrative structures that were already on the ground. The British acceptance of local leadership, when it was found, was a matter of practicality. Without a doubt, in time the British improved, if not perfected, the local indigenous ethnic administration. The chieftain system became a powerful tool of native administration, and the agent of the state in collecting taxes from the natives. This new system also became the powerful enforcer of the rule of law.

For Arop Biong, and the two or three generations of his children who followed him into the leadership of the Ngok Dinka of Abyei, the issues they had to contend with were much larger than those that were being dealt with by their contemporaries to the south. For instance, the leadership of the Ngok Dinka had to contend with slavery, and the abduction of Dinka women and children, and even men, into the Arab slave trade.

Chief Arop Biong had to deal with the Mahdia, the first Islamic revolution in Sudan which was led by Mohamed Ahmed al Mahdi. Al Mahdi left Khartoum for Western Northern Sudan, Kordofan and Darfur, to organize his army from the natives of those areas, in order to evict the Turko-Egyptian invaders of Sudan. Al Mahdi's revolutionary excursion into Western Sudan was not only successful; it was swift.

This was a revolution that was largely staged amongst the Arabs and Muslims of Western Sudan. The natives in these areas needed no persuading to become a native army that could repulse foreign invaders. But the number of Western Sudanese Arabs was small, and al Mahdi needed as many men as he could get. So he travelled southwards to Muglad, the southernmost tip of the Arab territory. For Chief Alor Biong and his Ngok Dinka people of Abyei, the Mahdia was not distant but domestic news. If the Messiria Baggara Arabs welcomed the Mahdi into their midst and were readily joining the Mahdia army, the Ngok had to do the same.

So Chief Alor Biong and selected subordinate elders travelled to meet al Mahdi some distance north of Abyei. They feared that if they did not gather gifts and offerings they could be suspected of resisting; it was prudent to do the right thing. The Dinka found the names of the places in Messiria Baggara Arab country, and therefore in Northern Sudan, difficult to remember, let alone pronounce accurately. Although there are suggestions that al Mahdi actually reached South Sudan, such accounts are difficult to corroborate.

One story told amongst the Ngok Dinka was that when their chief and his followers arrived at the place where they were to be introduced to al Mahdi, it was prayer time. When he started to lead the prayers and the Muslims lined up behind him to pray, Chief Alor Biong and Chief Jipur Alor of the Ngok Dinka of Abyei joined in. But of course they knew nothing about Islam! Even so, they perfectly imitated the Islamic prayer ritual to appear to be true Muslims. Whilst the Ngok chiefs were bending their heads down in prayer, Jipur Alor, one of Alor Biong's confidants, asked the chief, while their heads were hitting the ground: 'Do you see God now that you are bending down like that?' Alor Biong ordered Jipur to keep quiet, telling him that not every ques- tion that comes to mind should be asked. Nevertheless, the trip to meet

the Mahdi was successful. How much it influenced the attitude of the
Ngok Dinka chiefs when it came to joining the North is difficult to say.

Each generation has its own way of dealing with problems. The
blame put on traditional leaders by the new generation of Ngok is
not totally justified. While good neighbourliness lasted, the Ngok
community enjoyed peace and tranquillity between themselves and the
Messiria Baggara Arabs. Even the British colonial administrators saw
how traditionally unruly the Messiria were and how intransigent the
Dinka could be. How to strike a balance between these difficult neighbours was always problematic for the British. Even the naming of rivers
and areas had to be taken very seriously.

It was clear to the British colonial officials that it was not easy to
make decisions that would be readily acceptable to both sides. It was
difficult, for instance, to decide that a pasture or a stream belonged to
this or that community without being accused of favouring one ethnic
group over the other. As a more detailed example, let us return to the
need for the Baggara Arabs to move southwards with their livestock
during the dry months of the year, between December and April, to
graze and water their animals on what was obviously Dinka land. At
first, the colonial officials searched the area close to the Arab permanent settlement in order to discover whether or not it could sustain the
Arabs without their encroachment on the Dinka land. In those old days
of better rainfall, the British at first mistook some of the streams which
arose during the rainy season and stayed full of water until the next
rainfall for true rivers, and called them Bahr el Arab, 'the river of the
Arabs'. But the Baggara Arabs knew the area much better, and insisted
that the real river was further south. The colonial officials kept shifting
the name of Bahr el Arab southwards, until the name finally landed on
the present River Kiir.

The Dinka have never forgiven the British for giving their river
an Arab name. But the reason for this was not because the British
favoured the Baggara Arabs over the Dinka; rather, it was that the
British suspected that if the Dinka name was retained, the Dinka would
not allow the Baggara Arabs to seasonally migrate. And if the Baggara
Arabs had migrated to the river anyway, this being a vital necessity
for them and their livestock, there would surely have been countless

conflicts between the two communities. There was absolutely no way the colonial administration, or any administration, could fail to decide in favour of unrestricted seasonal migration by the Baggara Arabs to the River Kiir during the dry season. Such restriction of movement would have resulted in the massive loss not only of livestock, but also of the Arabs themselves.

Even so, giving the river an Arab name has not brought peace between these two ethnic communities of Southern Kordofan; far from it. There are tribal feuds, if not wars, between the Baggara Arabs of Kordofan and Darfur and the Dinka up until the present day.

While the Sudan remained a single country under colonialism, and both national administration and local colonial administration in the provinces and the districts were strong and effective, these policies worked, up to a point. Although those on both sides argued, making claims and counter-claims, the river was used by both parties, with relatively little rancour. The current problem between the two ethnic communities arose with the surge in political problems.

As far as the presence of the Ngok Dinka of Abyei in Kordofan is concerned, problems did not arise until South Sudanese political claims became part of the political, geographical, cultural and racial divide between the South and the North of what had since the Juba conference of 1947 really become one Sudan. At that conference the colonial civil secretary, James Robertson, decided, without any consideration of how the people of the two parts would treat each other, that Southern Sudan had to be considered a single country with Northern Sudan.

After Sudan become independent in 1956, Robertson was trans-ferred from Khartoum to Lagos, Nigeria, and became that country's last governor-general before it became independent. It was there that he helped to create one of the only functioning federations in Africa, this clearly being the best way of managing the feuding nationalities.

I came to know Sir James Robertson after I became Sudan minister of culture and information, and had many discussions with him about what might have been if he had created a federation between Northern and South Sudan as part of his decision to amalgamate the two Sudans at the 1947 conference. He told me that he had never served in South

Sudan during any part of his long colonial service in the country, but that his Northern Sudanese political friends, some of whom he took with him to Juba to attend the conference, were all honourable people. He told me that they had assured him they would look after the people of South Sudan. Yet the country is now two, as a result of one side failing to look after the other. If equality of opportunities and participation had been created, perhaps human failures might have been mitigated and the country could have remained one.

Sir James Robertson was at one point the colonial district commissioner for Western Kordofan, with his headquarters at Nahud. He has written in his memoirs about the Ngok Dinka people of Abyei and their chief, Kuol Arop, and also told me quite a few stories about his dealings with the Ngok chief that cannot be part of this work.

Relations between Southern Sudan as it was known and Northern Sudan did not became normal until the South split away to become the Republic of South Sudan. An example of these abnormal relations is the situation surrounding slavery. When slavery was abolished by Britain, this decision applied to its overseas colonies as well. However, in the case of Sudan, some unscrupulous Northern Sudanese slave merchants continued to smuggle South Sudanese slaves to the North, and because the border between North and South could not be controlled and managed – it is some 2,000 miles long and very porous – the British closed the border of South Sudan to the Northern Sudanese traders, decreeing a law called 'closed district ordinance'. Any Northern Sudanese who wanted to travel to South Sudan from the North were required to obtain written permission before they could travel, unless they were employees of the government of Sudan. The Northern Sudanese interpreted this restriction of travel to the South as separation of the South from the North. But before 1947 there had not been unity between the South and the North anyway.

It is difficult to be specific about when relations between the Ngok Dinka of Abyei and their Messiria Baggara Arab neighbours began to deteriorate. What is clear is that as the South Sudanese began to articulate their political cause and were joined by the few educated Ngok Dinka of Abyei, especially those who had been educated in South

Sudanese schools, the Messiria Baggara Arabs became more and more hostile to the Ngok people, who were very much part of their shared administration.

From 1965, when the first recorded bloody conflict between the Messiria Baggara Arabs and the Ngok occurred, there was a continuous massacre of the Ngok people by the Baggara Arabs. The last and the most serious such massacre took place in Babanousa, a railway town of Southern Kordofan. More than a thousand Dinka, not only from Abyei, were barricaded into railway wagons, and these were then set on fire. From that time, any Dinka, including students and schoolchildren, many of whom had previously travelled between Abyei and other parts of Northern Sudan, were offloaded from any form of transport they were using and massacred.

The problem of the Ngok Dinka of Abyei truly became a security problem. This is why it became impossible for the liberation movements of South Sudan, the current SPLM, which now rules South Sudan, and the Anya-Nya liberation movement before it, to ignore the Abyei issue, even though Abyei was never previously an issue in the political conflict during which South Sudan finally became an independent country, without Abyei.

As already related here, Abyei became part of Northern Sudan on the insistence of its own traditional leaders. The political elite of South Sudan had to be careful in their handling of the Abyei situation – not indicating that they wanted it to be an independent state, but also having a hidden ambition to separate geographical parts of Northern Sudan because of their strong cultural and blood affinity with the South.

The way to resolve the Abyei problem, the way to make Abyei part of the Republic of South Sudan, if that is what the people want, is not to spin the problem into a war between two neighbours, in the way the SPLM and their friends abroad want to present it. This is a policy that will guarantee Abyei will never become part of South Sudan. This is simply because Abyei was not taken by Northern Sudan from the South by force. Only what is taken from you by force, because you were weak, should be pursued by force until it is retrieved, no matter how long this takes. Whoever is weak today may become strong tomorrow, and may be able to get back what was taken by force.

The only reason why South Sudan should pursue their case with the North peacefully, until the Ngok people become citizens of South Sudan, is because the Northern Sudanese political elite and the Messiria Baggara Arabs of Southern Kordofan have shown that they are not interested in safeguarding and looking after the welfare of the Ngok people.

Moreover, the CPA Abyei protocol is a binding agreement between Khartoum and Juba and needs to be implemented. Since the Ngok people are just across the border from their Dinka kith and kin, Juba should do everything possible, short of war, to return the Abyei people to South Sudan. To achieve this, Juba first needs to normalize its relationship with Khartoum. Whoever rules Khartoum when the Abyei issue is finally resolved, Juba will be dealing with Khartoum, and will need to be regarded as a good neighbour, not interested in mischief. In the meantime, Juba must also correct the mistakes it has made within its political system and structures, as these alarm Khartoum and give it cause to think that whatever steps Juba takes over Abyei are intended to be confrontation and war.

The problem of the Ngok Dinka of Abyei is not the only issue confronting Juba in its relationship with Khartoum. There are several other problems that make cooperation difficult. For example, the revolutionary zeal of the SPLM against Khartoum – which lasted some twenty-one years while the war went on between the two – has yet to dissipate. At the moment, Khartoum is accusing Juba of continuing to support Khartoum's rebels. Only when relations between Khartoum and Juba are normalized will the Dinka Ngok people of Abyei be able to hope for some resolution of their predicament.

There are at least two unresolved problems relating to the 2005 peace agreement between the two countries. The CPA of 2005 eventually resulted in an independent South Sudan. It also had a separate protocol for the Nuba Mountains of Southern Kordofan and the Angesina Hills of Southern Blue Nile, both part of Northern Sudan. Like the Abyei protocol, this was aimed at leading two regions of Northern Sudan to some form of self-rule. The protocol stated that popular consultations should be conducted amongst the people of these two areas, but these have yet to be held. The result is that these regions are still in a sort of war with Khartoum. Because Juba has not clearly and formally broken off its connection with them, Khartoum continues to accuse Juba of continuing to support the fighters there with arms and supplies. Indeed, Khartoum also accuses Juba of supporting rebels in the Darfur conflict. In the same way, since December 2013, when there was a coup attempt by the former vice-president of South Sudan, Riek Machar Teny, to overthrow the government, Juba has been accusing Khartoum of supporting Mr Machar against the South Sudanese government.

Because the relationship between Khartoum and Juba is so bad, it is now difficult to refute charges about the support of rebels by one side or the other.

The failure by Khartoum and Juba to cooperate over the Abyei referendum is a serious failure on both sides. It has made it difficult, if not impossible, to implement the Abyei protocol, which is the only direct action that will provide the answer to this very long, nagging problem.

The leaders of the Dinka Ngok people of Abyei, also, let us not forget, leaders of the SPLM, have not made matters any easier for their own people. They have an incredible notion that they can impose a solution to the Abyei problem without the cooperation of Khartoum – and think the world will support them. On many occasions, they have attempted to take over the territory called Abyei by force and to annex it to South Sudan, but have failed. In 2013 they conducted a fake referendum in Abyei without the support of Juba or Khartoum, although clearly Juba provided funding and logistics. They now think that the international community should recognize the result of that illegitimate referendum and should annex Abyei to South Sudan by force.

The government in Juba is at least guilty of supporting a one-sided administration of Abyei by continuing to fund it without the support of Khartoum. This illegitimate administration wants Juba to occupy Abyei by force – a kind of declaration of war with Khartoum. The only legitimate solution, if the international community is still interested in anything legitimate for South Sudan, is to conduct the promised Abyei referendum.

Apart from what I learned at the Abyei Dinka chiefs' conference in 1952, I also know that my father tried time and again to persuade Chief

Deng Majok Kuol to return with his people to the South. My father and the chief had been contemporaries, and were initiated to manhood together on the same day. As chiefs of adjacent areas they had many things in common and exchanged visits regularly.

At the Abyei meeting which I attended with my father, I know that my father and Chief Deng Majok Kuol stayed awake for long hours each night – with my father not only reviewing the meeting of the day, but also urging the chief to return his people to the South.

For my father, the fact that the Ngok was now part of Northern Sudan rather than South Sudan had become a personal problem. Before Chief Arop Biong decided to become part of Northern Sudan, with his people, the legend has it that my people, Kuac Anganya, now better known as Kuac Madut Ring, were one people with them. The Ngok and the Kuac have their heads marked in the same way. My father and Chief Deng Majok Kuol were head-marked together on the same day, at my ancestral home, during their initiation rite. The Ngok say that for spiritual reasons and reasons of succession into chieftainship, Chief Deng Majok Kuol had to be head-marked again after he had returned to Abyei from Kuac, to entitle him to the chieftainship of the Ngok Dinka and to the personal possession of the spiritual spears of his ancestors.

Chapter 2

The 1952 Abyei Conference: The Last Attempt to Return the Ngok People to the South

Although the British colonial civil servants running South Sudan were not persuaded by the position taken by the Arop Biong family to keep the Ngok Dinka of Abyei in Northern Sudan, there was very little they could have done to change that situation without the consent of the Ngok Dinka chiefs, as they were largely subordinate to Northern Sudanese officials.

By 1947, with the British civil secretary in charge of the colonial administration of Sudan in Khartoum having decided that South Sudan was now one country with Northern Sudan, the dice were finally cast against the Ngok people of Abyei. With such glaring administrative discrimination by the British against the South, there was hardly anything to persuade the Ngok chiefs, especially their head chief (by this time Deng Majok Kuol Arop), to change their attitude and to allow their people to return to their kith and kin in the South. There had already been such administrative ill-treatment of the South that the Ngok chiefs thought the disadvantages they would be facing there indicated they should choose to remain part of the North.

A small example will demonstrate what the Ngok Dinka chiefs kept by remaining part of Northern Sudan. One of the advantages was in salary, there being a world of difference between the earnings of chiefs in Northern Sudan and in South Sudan. The reason for this disparity was because chiefs' salaries were a percentage of the local taxes paid into the public treasury, and the population in Northern Sudan paid more taxes to the public coffer than could be afforded by the South.

Local taxes in Northern Sudan were raised on every property an individual citizen possessed, immoveable and moveable, including livestock and other animals. In South Sudan taxation was only per male, called 'poll tax', and was very minimal at that. Even though the taxation levied on a Ngok man was equivalent to that levied on a South Sudanese man, the Ngok chief could not be persuaded to give up the advantages he enjoyed by being part of Northern Sudan.

There were also much more tenable administrative concerns, mentioned elsewhere in this book, which made it difficult for the Ngok chief to return to the South before independence came to Sudan. Besides, with the British having made up their mind about where the South as a whole belonged – with Northern Sudan as a single country – there was no reason for the local Ngok leadership to think that anyone would separate South Sudan from the North after independence.

So, in 1952, when the British decided to convene a final conference to persuade Chief Deng Majok Kuol Arop to agree for his people to be returned to the South from the North, to be part of Bahr el Ghazal and to be administered from there, alongside the Dinka community, Chief Deng Majok Kuol Arop emphatically turned down the offer. I personally attended every session of that February–March 1952 conference, and can almost relate the details of it verbatim. When the conference took place in Abyei I was an eleven- or twelve-year-old junior secondary school pupil. My father had taken notice of my keen interest in public matters and had taken me along with him. At this point it was not a political matter, but rather an administrative concern. Because it was the last chance for the Ngok Dinka of Abyei to return to the South, the British invited all the Dinka chiefs from across South Sudan to try to persuade Chief Deng Majok Kuol Arop. Session after session in the five-day conference, they all failed.

Although the conference ended in failure, the colonial administrators did not want to admit, there and then, that this was the case. It is clear that colonial administrators such as Governor Richard Owen of Bahr el Ghazal clearly saw no future for the people of Abyei in the North, because he saw no real future for the entire people of South Sudan in a united South and North. The governor wrote in his hand-over notes to his successor, his former deputy governor, that he could not see any of the Northern Sudanese Arab administrators successfully administering the Dinka people. Events have proven him right, and the people of Abyei continue to suffer and face an uncertain future.

After the Abyei conference, Chief Deng Majok Kuol Arop was given three months in which to finally make up his mind, and was invited to tour the Dinka districts of Bahr el Ghazal to observe how Dinka chiefs all over South Sudan administered their own people autonomously, without much interference from the colonial administration. The chief travelled to Gogrial, Aweil, Wau, Tonj, Rumbek and Yirol, but still refused to decide to return his people to South Sudan.

It might be inferred that the British left it too late in the day to persuade the chief. These events were only taking place because members of the South Sudanese political elite were raising some noise about the necessity for federal arrangements between South Sudan and Northern Sudan before the British could leave Sudan.

The British had already given their word at the 1952 Cairo conference between Britain and Egypt, as colonial condominium authority over Sudan, that Sudan would become independent, with a unitary system of government. Northern Sudan was represented at this conference by its political elite, and they threw their lot in with Egypt for the institutionalization of immediate independence for Sudan.

Because the Northern Sudanese political elite had promised Cairo they would consider immediate union between Sudan and Egypt as soon as Sudan became independent, the Egyptian authorities threatened to unilaterally withdraw from Sudan as a colonial power if Britain contemplated any possible delay in independence for Sudan because of the situation in South Sudan. With so much of interest for Britain elsewhere in the Middle East – the Suez Canal in Egypt and the control of the oil-rich Gulf states, for example – there was no way they could hesitate or delay events in the interests of South Sudan. Clearly, Britain's short- and long-term interests were with Northern Sudan and the Middle East, and not with South Sudan and Africa.

Even after the South Sudanese military garrison of the Sudan Defence Force mutinied at Torit in Eastern Equatoria in August 1955, in order to send a message to Britain about its disappointment with the way the takeover of power from the British had gone, the British governor general, Sir Robert Howe, in effect still in charge of the political affairs of colonial Sudan, sent a very clear message to the South Sudanese commanders that there was nothing Britain could do, and that the South Sudanese rebels had to 'face the consequences of their own action like men'.

The leaders of this first South Sudanese rebellion against the newly instituted national government of Sudan decided that they were taking part in what was in effect a liberation struggle for South Sudan. A few surrendered to the regime of the day and were immediately executed without due process. Many others took to the bush in South Sudan, regrouped and reorganized, but waited for the political outcome of the debate about federal arrangements that was taking place in Khartoum, having been promised to the South in the self-governing parliament on 19 December 1955 as a price for the South to vote for independence on 1 January 1956. The North reneged on the federation promise, and the first civil war of Sudan began in earnest.

Since the people of Abyei had not called on their local leadership to return Abyei to the South, and since there were no signs of political or security disturbances in Abyei up to this point, the assumption became that the people of Abyei were happy to remain part of Northern Sudan. Naturally, even the debate about federation between Northern Sudan and South Sudan had assumed that when political borders were eventually demarcated, the only point of reference for them would be the colonial provincial borders between the six provinces of Northern Sudan and the three provinces of South Sudan: Bahr el Ghazal, the closest province to Abyei; Equatoria, the only province of South Sudan that had no border with Northern Sudan; and Upper Nile, which, like Bahr el Ghazal, had an extensive border with Northern Sudan.

As the political debate about federal arrangements between South Sudan and Northern Sudan raged on, it clearly sent a misleading message to many people in South Sudan, particularly the Ngok people of Abyei: that South and North Sudan were settling down as a single united country. Any call for federal arrangements was not a big enough deal that it would force the Ngok people of Abyei to take a stand one way or the other.

However, when regrouping was taking place after the failed August 1955 armed struggle, and the South Sudanese rebels named themselves the Anya-Nya Liberation Movement, a few members of the Ngok Dinka community of Abyei joined their ranks. Most of these people had been educated in schools in South Sudan, so much so that most people, from both the North and South, and including the Ngok Dinka themselves, assumed that what they were doing was a personal preference, rather than a desire to return the Dinka people of Abyei from Northern Sudan to the South.

When countries in colonial Africa became independent, the demarcation of geographical borders was not the same as the demarcation of citizenship for individuals, as I have mentioned before. It was easy to assume, therefore, that any Ngok Dinka citizen from Abyei who had joined the rebellion in the South, while the country was still one, could choose to become a citizen of a new country, without that individual choice of citizenship affecting the land borders and the remaining group citizenship. So if Sudan (the original country) and South Sudan (the new country) were cooperating in the demarcation of their original borders, the 1 January 1956 border, which is now the legal border between Sudan and South Sudan, cannot be affected by individual citizens of any of the areas whose situation has not yet been resolved. There are legal processes by which the two states can resolve how and where individual citizens belong. A Dinka Ngok citizen of Abyei, a territory that is clearly Northern Sudan in accordance with 1 January 1956, who wants to become a citizen of the Republic of South Sudan can do so by following legal procedures, without those procedures being muddled up with messy geographical border politics.

For nearly a hundred years, the Ngok people seemed happy that Abyei was in Kordofan, Northern Sudan. Important political decisions had been taken in the interest of the affected communities, and to change such decisions the communities needed to have a say, rather than their leaders taking up guns and dictating their decisions.

What changed the situation for the Ngok Dinka of Abyei was clearly the political upheaval between South Sudan and the ruling elite of Northern Sudan. The latter simply decided that South Sudan had been a political gift to the North by the British, and that the South had no right of equal participation in the management of the political affairs and social life of the country. Looking at the situation in these terms, it can be said, with much justification, that the North forced South Sudan to rebel. The people of Abyei found themselves forced to make a decision to be with the South or with the North. Unfortunately, even such a vital decision that affects the life and future of the people has not proved to be clear cut.

Those leaders of the Ngok Dinka community who took part in the liberation struggle of South Sudan believe that the majority of the Ngok Dinka have decided they want to return their territory and people to South Sudan. But that is only a political statement. On the other hand, there is a sizeable group of people from Abyei who argue that it is in their best interest to stay put in Northern Sudan. They argue that the Ngok Dinka territory belongs to Northern Sudan. How many there are of these people does not really matter, and would only do so if the leaders who are running South Sudan from Juba and Northern Sudan from Khartoum agree on a political solution. An agreement like this is so distant that it is not easy to believe that a solution is particularly close, or indeed feasible at all.

What has been compounding the problem of arriving at a solution? The answer to this lies in the extremely muddled politics of the two countries, and the severely entrenched positions which both governments have developed, abetted by those on both sides who want to hold their government allies hostage.

If Khartoum does not stop acting as an agent for the Messiria Baggara Arab tribe, and instead acts as the guardian and protector of Sudan and all its people, it will be difficult to reach a solution for Abyei. The same applies to the government in Juba, which is clearly being held hostage by the handful of Ngok Dinka leaders of the SPLM, who seem to think and behave as if without them there would have been no South Sudan. This group, which is dominated by a small handful of the late Chief Deng Majok Kuol Arop's children, behave with incredible arrogance, and continue to believe that they can coerce South Sudan to liberate Abyei by force of arms, since for them it is obvious that the SPLM leadership follows their dictates.

The SPLM leadership of South Sudan, generally and not just the leaders of Abyei alone, has made it clear that they think they know everything, and that matters can only be resolved their way. This is causing problems, not only with neighbours such as Sudan, but even amongst themselves. The current war that is raging in South Sudan is an internal conflict within the one ruling party; only people who do not wish to accurately describe the situation are calling it a civil war. Look at the role of the leaders of Abyei. Deng Alor Kuol, the leader of that Ngok community group within the SPLM, was for a long time the darling of the late Colonel John Garang de Mabior and is also popular with the current leader of South Sudan, Salva Kiir Mayardit. He is the leader of the rebel group within the SPLM leadership, the group that tried to overthrow the elected President Salva Kiir Mayardit of South Sudan by force of arms and failed.

In one of Deng Alor Kuol's recent antics, he returned to South Sudan, on the coat-tails of the vice-president of South Africa, Cyril Ramaphosa, posing as the leader of a rebel group. He made a brash statement at Juba airport to waiting journalists, to the effect that the rebellion's leaders had returned to save the country, because President Salva Kiir Mayardit's government had failed. But because Deng Alor Kuol had no confidence to remain and stay in South Sudan without foreign protection, he left on the vice-president of South Africa's plane, in order to live abroad. This is the man who wants to resolve the problems of the people of Abyei.

The Abyei situation requires much more prudent leadership than is being provided by Deng Alor Kuol, Luka Biong Deng Majok Kuol or retired General Pieng Deng Majok Kuol. Their attitude has made resolution of the Abyei case rather difficult. Is it war that they want to pursue? Or is it the implementation of the referendum provided for by the CPA? And can Khartoum be kept out of any resolution of the Abyei problem and still arrive at a credible solution? It would seem that the elders of the Ngok community – who have now passed on – had a much better plan for the welfare of their community than those who currently masquerade as war heroes.

Staying in the North under Chief Deng Majok Kuol Arop had, for a very long time, maintained peace between the entire Dinka community and the Messiria Baggara Arabs. Deng Majok Kuol Arop became a distinguished leader, not just of his Ngok Dinka section of Abyei, but for the entire Southern Kordofan, a proud territory of Northern Sudan.

Deng Majok Kuol Arop interchanged the local native court presidency with Messiria Baggara Arab chiefs, of the like of Babo Nimir. Even when he was not the president of the local Messiria Baggara Arabs and the Ngok Dinka joint native court of Abyei, the Arabs had to comply completely with his instructions when they moved south with their cattle to graze and water along the River Kiir. The Arabs normally went back home to Northern Sudan with their livestock during the rainy season, as there was enough pasture and water there, and the Arab cattle were said not to be rugged enough to endure the heavy rain of the Dinka country, or its mud and mosquitoes.

Similarly, there are times of the year, mainly towards the end of the rainy season, when not only the Ngok Dinka but also the other Dinka to the south, mainly in northern Bahr el Ghazal, Gogrial and Aweil, need to move with their cattle to the north. Northern Sudan is a much drier territory than South Sudan, with lush pasture and water holes. The land in the Sudd of South Sudan would just be beginning to dry from the rains. Chief Deng Majok Kuol Arop had authorization from the Dinka chiefs of Bahr el Ghazal to look after their people on their behalf. These smooth and peaceful arrangements worked very well, and enhanced the authority and the power of the local chiefs. Deng Majok Kuol Arop imposed fines on the Dinka from Bahr el Ghazal and on the Baggara Arabs in equal measure. Unfortunately, there is no longer an authority that imposes law and order or keeps the peace. The whole situation is a disaster for the two communities that live in this area.

The idea that only Khartoum or Juba know what is best has made it much more difficult to ensure security for the local population. Abyei has had to be evacuated each time there is an SPLA military offensive in the area. Unfortunately, these offensives have had dire consequences for the Ngok people and for Abyei as a Ngok community area.

Abyei is currently an occupied territory, along with the territory of the Twic Mayardit Dinka community south of Abyei, the occupier being an Ethiopian contingent of the United Nations Peacekeeping Force. But there is no peace. The Ethiopians have become a UN occupation force, issuing their own orders to the local population and committing violent acts with impunity. This foreign force, imposed by Deng Alor Kuol when he was South Sudan's minister for foreign affairs, has made life intolerable for the local population, Ngok and others.

Chief Kuol Adol Deng Majok Kuol Arop was ambushed and killed by the Messiria Baggara Arabs while he was travelling on a UN-marked armoured truck on 4 May 2013. No one dared arrest the Messiria Arabs who were involved, even though they were identified and well known. Is this the type of peace that Deng Alor Kuol Arop and the children of Chief Deng Majok Kuol Arop, who are leaders of the SPLM and rulers of South Sudan in Juba, want to impose on their own people? These young leaders of the Ngok Dinka, whenever they want to demonstrate their power, order units of unprepared SPLA soldiers to drive into Abyei, have a shoot out, then ride back to Juba. These leaders do not even accompany the SPLA troops to Abyei, even though they are all active serving SPLA commanders. They are afraid, in case any of them get caught in an ambush. They simply issue orders and remain in Juba, 1,000 miles from Abyei.

Meanwhile, the Messiria Baggara Arabs defy the Ethiopian military force occupying Abyei, and consider themselves to be at war with the occupiers. The Messiria are only answerable to Khartoum, and Khartoum in turn is happy that the Arabs are causing havoc in Abyei in their name.

Now, Deng Alor Kuol Arop – interested only in the exercise of power in South Sudan in order to receive the benefits of that power – has returned to office in Juba as Minister of Foreign Affairs as part of the 'peace process' that has not restored any peace to South Sudan. The so-called peace agreement of August 2015 is not working in South Sudan because it is not a peace agreement between the South Sudanese parties to the conflict, but it is a foreign-imposed peace agreement on the people of South Sudan, following the failure of Deng Alor Kuol and Riek Machar Teny to overthrow the elected government of South Sudan in their December 2013 coup attempt.

Chapter 3

The Abyei Situation and South Sudan

By 1965, following the popular overthrow of the first military dictatorship in the country, the Abboud regime in Khartoum, the situation of the Ngok Dinka of Abyei had already been forced onto the political lap of South Sudan. The Southern Front had organized itself into a very credible, if not a formidable, political force, and was now represented in the interim government of Sudan, under Sir el Khatim el Khalifa, the interim prime minister. The Southern Front had sold the idea of a round table conference to the government of the day to discuss South Sudan with a view to finding a political solution to this problem, which was already a civil war of long standing – over eleven years. At the onset of the twelve-month interim period, the Southern Front had initiated a series of political initiatives which it had committed to accomplish during the interim period:

> First, the government of the day had to hold a round table conference to discuss a political solution to the problem of the South.

> Second, the round table conference had to be held outside Sudan in another African country, preferably in East Africa, because the leadership of the Anya-Nya liberation movement of South Sudan was based there and it was thought they should attend the conference.

> Third, there would be no election in the country before a political solution to the problem of South Sudan was found. A general election had to be conducted within twelve months during the interim period. That was the interim government's real constitutional and

political mandate. Since such a political mandate of running the general election in the country could not be carried out without security, it made sense that the Southern Front called for the convening of a round table conference.

The government of Prime Minister Sir el Khatim el Khalifa accepted the holding of a round table conference and prepared for it. These preparations were watched over by a three-man member team from the Southern Front, which also had to get on with other matters of policy for South Sudan before the conference, including convening its first national convention at Malakal, the capital of Upper Nile province of South Sudan.

At the Malakal convention, the Southern Front approved the tabling of the right of South Sudan to self-determination. This was a watershed policy for the South and indeed for the whole of Sudan. In those days, even a call for federation was a treasonable offence from the point of view of the Northern Sudanese political elite.

Ezbon Mundiri, one of the bravest South Sudanese political thinkers of the time, had been denied his seat in the Sudanese parliament of 1957 because he stood in his Maridi constituency under the slogan of federation between the South and the North. Even though he was elected, he was charged with treason and sentenced to twenty years in prison with hard labour. The Southern Front released him in October 1964, following the overthrow of the Abboud regime, and nominated him as one of the Southern Front's three cabinet ministers in the 1964–5 interim government. His release and ministerial role were also a watershed in the politics of Sudan.

One of the issues that confronted the Southern Front at the Malakal convention, after the tabling of self-determination by the South at the Round Table Conference had been approved, was the issue of the borders between the South and the North. Being an intellectually led movement, the Southern Front always predicted the possible problems that would be experienced in dealing with Northern Sudan, and tried not to leave anything to chance. They felt that the Northern Sudanese political elite would attempt to encroach on South Sudanese land. The Malakal convention resolved that the South should settle on the borders with the North that were already well demarcated as provincial borders: the colonial borders of the nine provinces of Sudan.

Bahr el Ghazal borders two provinces of the North, Darfur and Kordofan. The second province of the South, Upper Nile, also has borders with two provinces of the North, Kordofan and Blue Nile. These borders would be difficult to disentangle, because they are inhabited by large populations from both sides, are pastoral lands for animal grazing and watering, and are fertile agricultural lands. With such occupancy, it is difficult to keep the communities away from them and from one another, which is precisely the difficulty that must be kept in mind when searching for an honest, genuine solution to the Abyei problem.

The need for an honest solution is still with us today. The tragedy of the Abyei situation is that it is difficult to sense that anyone is looking for a resolution that will satisfy both sides. An honest resolution is the only one that will last – nothing less, nothing more. Sadly, the political leadership on both sides is relying on force of arms and not on peaceful resolution, because neither wants a solution in which both sides win. Looking at the tactics currently being deployed, each side wants to be the only winner! And neither side is being truthful about the causes of the Abyei problem. How can it be true that Abyei as a geographical space belongs to the Messiria Baggara Arabs? And how can it be true that the Ngok Dinka land of Abyei is a contested land between Juba and Khartoum?

When the Southern Front decided to table the right of the South to self-determination, it had first to debate the circumstances in which it found itself. As stated above, one of the most important issues up for discussion was the border issue. As many delegates, especially from Bahr el Ghazal and Upper Nile, have common borders with the North, this debate was an emotional one.

Delegations from Bahr el Ghazal spoke bitterly about the annexation of the Kafia Kenji, a region of Western Bahr el Ghazal district of Raga, to Darfur in Northern Sudan. This is an area of South Sudan reputed to be rich with minerals, uranium and copper amongst others, which is why General Ibrahim Abboud decreed that the area was now part of Darfur. Darfur at this time was a loyalist province of Northern

Sudan, whose black African citizens were used by Khartoum as government soldiers to massacre South Sudanese citizens. Darfur could annex part of the territory of South Sudan without a problem, as far as the powers in Khartoum were concerned.

The Southern Front could have agreed that this matter would be settled by war, since war between the South and the North was already raging anyway. But, as political activists and thinkers, the leadership comprehensively engaged in broad thinking about peaceful resolution to the existing conflict, rather than making matters worse. All issues, therefore, including Abyei and Kafia Kenji, had to be discussed thoroughly at the Malakal convention.

So what was the Southern Front solution to the border issue? It is interesting to note how they predicted the problems around borders that are currently confronting the political leadership of South Sudan, the SPLM. To the Southern Front, the idea was to eliminate any stumbling blocks that were in the way of resolution of the Abyei situation. They predicted that the debate about Abyei would be a long one, and could in fact marginalize the political cause of South Sudan. The solution was therefore to deal first with what was doable, without giving up the right to pursue other problems.

Since Abyei was not taken by the North by force, and since at the time of the debate at Malakal the voice of the representatives of the people of Abyei was not as pronounced as it is today, the Southern Front convention decided to use the provincial borders that had been demarcated and administered by colonialism for sixty years, and would remain as they were on 1 January 1956, when the British handed over the country to Northern Sudan. It was not definite that the North would accept this, but nothing the South decided at this time was acceptable to the North anyway.

It was embarrassing for the North to reject this plan, since they had accepted these borders for the sixty years of colonial rule; although it must have been clear to the representatives of Northern Sudan at the conference that the South was stealthily reclaiming the borders that the North had been breaching, especially when it came to Kafia Kenji, which the Abboud regime had renamed Hofrat el Nahas, 'the copper hole' in Arabic.

After the March 1965 conference, even though it was inconclusive, political enlightenment and awareness became more prominent in South Sudan. The people of Abyei, for example, could see that it was time to rise up and be politically active.

It might have been possible to incorporate the problem of the Ngok Dinka of Abyei into the political cause of South Sudan, considering that the South Sudan political movement was contemplating separation, but 'realpolitik' was the name of the game.

The implementation process of the CPA between South Sudan and Northern Sudan over the last ten years, since 2005, has shown how difficult it is for Juba and Khartoum to work together to resolve the still outstanding political, economic and social issues between them, especially border issues such as Abyei. Clearly, Khartoum and Juba each start from the premise that they are right and the other side is wrong.

Khartoum states all the time that Abyei is part of Northern Sudan – a Messiria Baggara Arab land according to the border maps of 1 January 1956. No further considerations are looked at in order to arrive at a mutual agreement that will reorder the borders.

There are also the encroachments into South Sudan by the North to consider, which were made by the central government in Khartoum when the country was one. These must now be resolved in order to normalize relations. The best example of these concerns Hofrat el Nahas, mentioned above. There is also the tricky issue of Heglig (Panthou), a clear Dinka territory of Western Upper Nile in South Sudan, which Khartoum made into one of its most important oil depots when the country was one. The situation here, because of its oil, has been complicated by the greed and political ineptitude of the leaders of the SPLM.

The Ngok leaders took a rather dubious claim to the International Court of Arbitration in The Hague, Holland, claiming that Heglig was a Ngok Dinka land and part of Abyei. They lost the case. Unfortunately, because the Ngok leaders claimed it was a dispute between Abyei and Northern Sudan, but had no evidence to prove their case, the International Court of Arbitration ruled in favour of Khartoum. This arbitration has made it difficult for Panthou to return to the South, because the court has ruled that it belongs to Northern Sudan and not to Abyei. The consolation in this mistake is that at least the South can still hold Khartoum to the text of the CPA, which says that the borders between the South and the North are as they were on 1 January 1956. Clearly, Panthou is part of South Sudan, and old colonial maps of Sudan should resolve this. This is one of the many problems that the SPLM's Ngok leaders have caused for South Sudan.

Knowing the prevailing attitudes of both sides to the border issues, and with Heglig now an economic oil fortress in the hands of Khartoum, it is not easy to know how the matter will be resolved without much rancour. Already, the same SPLM leaders have twice attempted to occupy Heglig by force of arms, and have failed. The problem for South Sudan is that no one in Juba holds these Ngok leaders accountable for their misdeeds – indeed no one holds any SPLM leader accountable, period. They all act with impunity.

One of the most brazen acts by the activist members of the Ngok Dinka community of Abyei was their attempt twice to demarcate what they believed was the correct border between the Ngok and the Messiria Baggara Arabs – even though at that point the border demarcators had not specified it was the border between South Sudan and Northern Sudan, merely a boundary between the Ngok Dinka and the Messiria Baggara.

The Ngok first attempted to demarcate their border with the Messiria Baggara by force in 1965. The Arabs unleashed their fighters and evicted the Dinka from the border, massacring hundreds, if not thousands, of innocent members of the Ngok Dinka community, their bodies being left to rot in the desert. Among them were a number of university students, such as the bright young Majak Abiem Bagat and his colleagues. This tribal fighting between the Ngok Dinka of Abyei and the Messiria Arabs was soon caught up by the results of the June 1965 elections in Northern Sudan, which brought Mohamed Ahmed Mahgoub of the Umma Party to power as prime minister. Mahgoub declared in parliament that every educated South Sudanese was a rebel and should be liquidated.

In one single night, on 9 July 1965, more than 1,400 South Sudanese civilians were massacred in Juba town by the government army; and then more than seventy-six South Sudanese employees of the government of Sudan and hundreds of others were massacred at a wedding party in Wau town on the night of 11 July 1965. No one said anything about these atrocities, as the government was massacring its own citizens.

Since 1965 the wanton killing of the Ngok Dinka people of Abyei by the Messiria Baggara Arabs has intermittently continued. It is fair to state that some of these incidents are provoked by the Ngok people themselves, probably as an expression of frustration of the long years without a solution to their problem. Unfortunately, some of this frustration has been taken advantage of by the educated leaders of the Ngok people themselves, exploiting the plight of their own people to score cheap political points.

One of the most recent horrendous incidents was the wanton killing of the senior chief of the Ngok Dinka of Abyei by Messiria Baggara gunmen in 2013, which I mentioned in the previous chapter. A committed man of peace, Chief Kuol Adol Deng Majok Kuol Arop aspired, like his late father, Chief Deng Majok Kuol Arop, to find peace between his Dinka Ngok people and the Messiria Baggara Arabs. The murderers of this man of peace achieved their objective, extinguishing the little flame of peace that he represented. As is always the case after incidents like this, peace was thrown further away. At the time of writing, no movement on either side has really been established again.

Clearly, neither the Messiria Baggara Arabs nor the Ngok Dinka of Abyei really have the ability or the capacity to impose a solution on the other by force of arms. Yet both continue to insist that only their solution – a solution unacceptable to the other party – is the answer to the problem. Where are the so-called UN peacekeepers?

I have already spoken about the UN peacekeeping force that was introduced into Abyei by the Ngok leaders of the SPLM. Neither the Messiria Baggara Arabs or Khartoum have recognized the presence of this force, and rather than being helpful, the Ethiopians are now complicating matters. The military contingent has become caught up in matters of land, borders and even trade between the tribes amongst whom it is supposed to be keeping peace. Can such a development help to bring about peace? It is very doubtful. All that is occurring is the addition of another layer of power struggle between locals, and there are now multiple ineffectual power enclaves. The political and security situation for the Ngok Dinka remains extremely tenuous, while everyone vies for position.

Important developments have occurred on the political scene in Sudan that may arguably have heightened public awareness of the cause of the Ngok Dinka people of Abyei. This awareness has even become international, thanks to the educated Ngok people who joined the SPLM and fought for their cause alongside the other South Sudanese. Does this mean that a solution to the problem, which has wasted so much human life and material resources, is finally possible? It is difficult to advance a definitive answer to this question. Only time will tell.

In May 1983, one of the many military dictators of Sudan, Jaafar Mohamed Nimeiri, repealed the 1972 Addis Ababa Peace Agreement that he had signed with the South to end the war, and the South took up arms again. An appreciable number of educated members of the Ngok Dinka community of Abyei joined the liberation war of South Sudan against the North.

The case of the Ngok people of Abyei was always very clear. They could not remain part of Northern Sudan, even if there was no war between the South and the North and even if there were no atrocities committed by the North against the Ngok. Perhaps individual South Sudanese could fit into Northern Sudanese society, especially if they had no political views and political awareness, or if they denied their conscience and refused to recognize every unacceptable treatment meted out to all the people of Southern Sudanese origin in the North. But an entire community, such as the Ngok Dinka of Abyei, cannot fit into the society of Northern Sudan and be comfortable. A political resolution to the Abyei problem is not easy to contemplate, though, because it is tied up with the very real socio-economic interests of another people, the Messiria Baggara Arabs of Kordofan, whose means of livelihood are entangled with the problem.

So far, the approaches being made to find a solution are unrealistic. The Ngok Dinka of Abyei think that a solution to the wider conflict of South Sudan with the North ought also to solve the Abyei issue. Unfortunately, this is not necessarily so. The late leader of the liberation movement of South Sudan, Colonel John Garang de Mabior, whom no one can accuse of not having the people of Abyei close to his heart, found this out when he negotiated the CPA and had to sign a separate protocol for Abyei, in order to separate the issues. The current leaders of the Ngok Dinka people of Abyei were very close to Colonel Garang, so they will know that people were always told: 'The leader [chairman] of the movement knew what to do with the Abyei problem.' And when the chairman knew something in the SPLM, no one else could ever have an opinion on that matter. So Abyei became a special case that was in the hands of the leader.

Before the SPLA became a liberation force, fighting for the cause of South Sudan after 1983, the 1972 Addis Ababa peace agreement was in place between the South and the North. The principal negotiator for the government of Sudan was Abel Alier Wal Kwai, a respected and distinguished South Sudanese political thinker and lawyer who became minister for Southern Sudan Affairs under Nimeiri. Alier had previously been one of the legal architects of the Southern Front's policy of self-determination at the 1965 Round Table Conference in Khartoum.

One of the principal weaknesses of the Addis Ababa agreement with the North was that it concentrated political power on the central government of Sudan, granting South Sudan regional autonomy without power. This was not constitutional – a thing that eventually encouraged Nimeiri to abrogate the autonomy of the South.

The problem of Abyei was not totally absent from the mind of Abel Alier as he negotiated in 1972 at Addis Ababa. One of the recommendations of the agreement was that the Ngok Dinka people of Abyei would be asked in a plebiscite to decide whether or not they wanted to revert to South Sudan. This recommendation was never carried out, because the suggested autonomy for South Sudan fell victim to a Northern Sudanese plot to undermine it, beginning with Nimeiri himself, who signed it into law in the first place.

When Nimeiri resolved to negotiate the end of the seventeen-year civil war with the South in 1972, neither he nor those around him had much of a plan for a political process that would allow the South to share power with Northern Sudan. This arguably included the South Sudanese within the Nimeiri regime, Abel Alier and Joseph Ukel Garang, before Alier at the newly created Ministry for Southern

Affairs. This is in spite of the fact that the Nimeiri regime followed on after the March 1965 conference in Khartoum at which Agrey Jaden, the leader of the Anya-Nya Liberation Movement of South Sudan, had called for an outright separation of South Sudan from the North. The Southern Front had strongly articulated at the same conference the right of South Sudan for self-determination. Anyone who wanted to negotiate peace with the South after the 1965 Round Table Conference ought to have known that a settlement with the South needed a political agenda that offered something of substance both politically and constitutionally to the South. But not so the 1972 Addis Ababa peace negotiations.

Led by Abel Alier Wal Kwai, the Nimeiri regime only offered the South a rather loose and very weak system of self-rule – regional autonomy that had no powers and depended largely on Nimeiri's generosity. In such circumstances, it was difficult, if not impossible, to define the resolution of the Ngok Dinka people of Abyei case against the North. They had already been part of Northern Sudan for a very long time. The 1972 Addis Ababa agreement only mentioned the Abyei case in political and non-specific terms. It said that areas of the Northern Sudan with cultural affinity to South Sudan may be consulted on how and where they wanted to be governed. No one wanted the Ngok Dinka community of Abyei to be consulted, or even implied this.

The Abyei protocol of the CPA is very clear that it wants the Ngok Dinka people of Abyei to decide in a referendum as to whether or not they want to revert to South Sudan from the North.

Nimeiri wanted an agreement that would end the raging civil war with the South, which was already threatening the survival of his own military regime – which had only been in power for two years when he signed the Addis Ababa agreement into law. Attempts by Abel Alier to do something about Abyei failed, because of the strong opposition from the North, so Alier eventually brought Zacharia Bol Deng Majok Kuol, a medical doctor, into his government in Juba as South Sudan regional minister of health. This was a small step that did nothing to appease the people of Abyei, even though it alarmed the North, especially the Messiria Baggara Arabs. The South was now being suspected of expansionist intentions.

When Nimeiri finally abrogated the autonomy of South Sudan in May 1983 and forced a second civil war on the country, the Abyei contingent in the war of liberation had become larger than ever before. The problem was that the leadership of the SPLA under Colonel John Garang had not stated clearly what the war was all about, as far as South Sudan was concerned. The right of the people of South Sudan for self-determination was only enshrined in the final document of the negotiations much later, thanks to the CPA mediators. Protocol number one became a very strong counter to Khartoum's insistence that they would not accept a peace agreement with the South that did not recognize Islam as the religion of the Sudanese state.

Colonel Garang's initial policy as leader of the liberation movement was to fight to establish a 'New Sudan'. This slogan was responsible for the inclusion of the black African peoples of Northern Sudan – the people of the Nuba Mountains of Southern Kordofan and of the Angesina Hills of Southern Blue Nile – in the liberation movement. All wanted to fight to establish a 'New Sudan', in which the black African people who formed the majority in the country would be the rulers.

Was the Ngok Dinka contingent of the SPLA also fighting to establish a 'New Sudan', like the Nuba and the Angesina people? You bet they were. But nothing was ever clear in the SPLM/A at that time. Once the leader spoke that was it: what he said was law. And judging from their behaviour, the Ngok leaders of the SPLM would have seemed quite happy for a 'New Sudan' to be created by their liberation movement. This was contrary to the position of the bulk of the SPLA fighting men from South Sudan, who wanted to liberate the South from the North. As mere soldiers, who had no say in political matters, they made it abundantly clear to their leadership that they were fighting to liberate South Sudan from the North.

Colonel Garang was aware of this separatist sentiment in the movement. It was always expressed to him freely, whenever he had an opportunity to interact with his fighting men. It was common knowledge that when he was asked by his men how was it that the SPLM leadership was fighting to liberate the whole of Sudan instead of concentrating only on the liberation of South Sudan, Colonel Garang was always quoted as saying that they should just carry on fighting for the 'New Sudan' until they arrived at Kosti, on the border between South Sudan and Northern Sudan. Those who did not want to fight for the 'New Sudan' could stop there. Garang said he would carry on with whoever was left to complete the liberation of Sudan.

The 'New Sudan' political agenda was one of the most contentious issues between me and Colonel Garang, although we did not permit it to interfere with our normal relations. We exchanged views on the matter, but left it there at the end of the conversation. The harshest exchange between us was at the State Department in Washington DC in 1994. Colonel Garang was explaining to US diplomats in a meeting with the US Assistant Secretary of State for African Affairs, Herman Cohen, what the 'New Sudan' was all about. He had just come up with his theory of three intersecting circles representing the various regions and communities of Sudan, which he theorized would eventually unite as one 'New Sudan'. The three societies were the Northern Sudanese Arab people, the now rulers of Sudan; the marginalized black African people of Northern Sudan, the people of the Nuba Mountains, the people of the Angesina Hills of the Southern Blue Nile and the black African Muslim people of Darfur, in Western Sudan; and the struggling black African people of South Sudan, who wanted to break away from the Arab North. I cannot say how the US diplomats attending that meeting felt about Colonel Garang's circles and his explanation of them. I sat quietly throughout and did not utter a word.

Finally, Secretary Cohen, a friend, turned to me and asked for my view. I told him that as this was the chairman of the SPLM's meeting, I had nothing to say. Perhaps expecting me not to contradict him in public, Colonel Garang said I had his permission to speak. I thanked him, and then told him that his circles, the whole idea of a 'New Sudan', was confusing for the people of South Sudan. All I knew was that the people of South Sudan had been fighting all their lives to liberate themselves from Northern Sudan. To liberate the whole of Sudan in order to create a 'New Sudan' was therefore a contradiction in terms for them. Colonel Garang became visibly angry. He told me that the least the South Sudanese would get from his 'New Sudan' agenda was independence. I was not surprised that he regarded the independence of South Sudan as a small achievement. The bigger achievement for him was the liberation of the whole of Sudan, which would then become a 'New Sudan' under his leadership. The South Sudanese should then become comfortable in the 'New Sudan' under a black African leader, John Garang.

Surprisingly, many Northern Sudanese intellectuals thought the idea of creating a 'New Sudan' in which the South would be a component was a good idea, especially as it would end the civil war. Colonel Garang was, therefore, the most popular South Sudanese in Northern Sudan, because of his call for Sudan to stay a united country.

The situation of the people of the Nuba Mountains and of the Angesina Hills was understandable. They wanted to stay with the North in a united Sudan, new or old. They were unionists and did not want the South to break away. They had a dream that, one day, the black Africans of Sudan would rule the country, especially if South Sudan remained part of the country. What was surprising and has not been explained is why the leaders of the SPLA from Abyei were so hostile to the call of the South for self-determination when they said they had joined the SPLA to fight to be part of South Sudan. If the South accepted that it should remain part of Northern Sudan, to form one Sudan, old or new, there did not seem to be any sense in wanting Abyei to break away from Kordofan to join Bahr el Ghazal if these SPLA leaders were happy with Northern Sudanese subjugation of the South.

So many mistakes have been made over the problem of Abyei since the signing of the CPA that disentangling these mistakes has now become a big problem. To begin to do this, it is important to underscore what Colonel Garang achieved at the Navaisha peace negotiations in Kenya in 2005. By all accounts, the solution of a referendum for the people of Abyei was the best that could be hoped for, short of a continuing war over this problem. The Navaisha protocol for Abyei is better than Abel Alier's idea of a plebiscite, because his 1972 idea was not made part of the Addis Ababa Peace Agreement that ended seventeen years of civil war with the North. The Navaisha Abyei protocol is part of the CPA and is therefore better. However, the Navaisha protocol is difficult to implement because the SPLM leadership, which inherited the CPA from Colonel Garang after his untimely death in a helicopter crash in July 2005, have converted the CPA into an agreement of hostilities with

Khartoum, rather than courting Khartoum into a normal relationship in which the CPA can be implemented. A peace agreement can only be fully implemented in cooperation with the persons with whom one has signed it, but all the leaders of the SPLM from Abyei who became part of the government of South Sudan, or were part of the coalition government in Khartoum during the six-year interim period have behaved as if the only way to treat Khartoum is as a hostile enemy, not as a partner in peace. Khartoum got the inkling that the autonomous government of South Sudan was behaving as if it was an agent for foreign powers. During this period there were, of course, friends of the leaders of the SPLM in South Sudan who wanted regime change in Khartoum, rather than the smooth implementation of the CPA. Clearly, by hoping for a change of regime in Khartoum meant that the leaders of South Sudan, which included the leaders of Abyei, did not care about the CPA or what it contained for the South or for their own people of Abyei. As foreign minister of the Republic of Sudan during the interim period, Deng Alor Kuol went to Europe on an official mission of the government of Sudan, but returned to Khartoum carrying a hostile message from the European Union in Brussels to President Omar el Bashir, the head of state of Sudan, who had signed the CPA.

For six long years, Deng Alor Kuol and Luka Biong Deng Majok Kuol Arop were ministers of the government of Sudan, either in Juba or in Khartoum. Their only achievement was annoying Khartoum and preventing the implementation of the CPA. For these two sons of the late Chief Deng Majok Kuol Arop, and their brother Pieng Deng Kuol Arop (who was in the army), the regime in Khartoum was not worthy of implementing the CPA with them as a partner – that regime had to be changed.

One of the recurring mistakes made by the Ngok leaders of the SPLM is assuming that Abyei has to be won back by the South by force. This may result in a permanent loss of Abyei to its own people and to the South. Three times already, the SPLA, under the command of General Pieng Deng Majok Kuol Arop, when he was deputy chief of staff of the South Sudanese Army, has attacked Abyei. On three occasions Abyei town has been devastated by war, but lost to the North within a few days, if not a few hours.

Now, as part of the contest with the North, the Messiria Baggara Arabs are encamped in Ngok Dinka territory, almost immediately north of Abyei. The Messiria Baggara, whose only claim to Abyei traditionally is that they graze their cattle in the area seasonally, are now building permanent dwellings in Ngok Dinka country.

The worst mistake, which Khartoum now uses as an excuse not to normalize relations with the South, is that the leaders of the Ngok Dinka have entrenched themselves in the government of South Sudan and are the ones who control the government relationship with Khartoum. When Khartoum sees Deng Alor Kuol and Luka Biong Deng Kuol as the ministers in charge of the South, the immediate conclusion is drawn that war policy with the North is being designed, because of Abyei.

Northern Sudan is of course one of South Sudan's most important neighbours, in spite of Abyei. Much of the South is now openly murmuring about the damage the leaders of Ngok in the SPLM are causing to relations with the North. As would be expected, these murmurs sometimes break into more open debate.

For instance, Deng Alor Kuol had to give up a parliamentary seat of the national assembly of South Sudan in Juba to its rightful owner, because he took the seat from Tonj of Warrap state in the 2010 general election. Someone within the leadership of the SPLM wanted to accommodate Deng Alor as one of the SPLM leaders from Abyei, and this was done without proper consultation with the rightful owners of the seat. Occurrences like this make sympathy for a deserving cause such as Abyei fade away from the hearts and minds of those whom Abyei needs so badly in order to return to the South in peace.

One of the severest mistakes made by the SPLM leaders is the brazen attempt to internationalize the Abyei problem. According to the wishes of Deng Alor Kuol, Luka Biong Deng Majok Kuol, General Pieng Deng Majok Kuol and their cohorts from Abyei in the SPLM leadership, the Abyei cause now has to be handled internationally. But can a solution be found via this route? Could a workable international solution be imposed on the Messiria Baggara Arabs and be acceptable? Would the government of Sudan in Khartoum and the Messiria Baggara Arabs give their consent? It is almost impossible to imagine how an imposed solution could work. If one needs to sway the opinion

Arabs riding horses. (From *The Man Called Deng Majok*, through the courtesy
and generosity of the author, Francis Mading Deng Majok Kuol Arop)

of others who have a claim on the situation, should one not start with
them?

On their part, the Messiria Baggara Arabs have overreached
themselves by claiming that Abyei as a territory belongs to them.
This is clearly false. I grew up in this area and when I was a child it
was always unlikely that one would see a Baggara Arab in this area
before December of any year. It was only during the dry season that
we saw them on their horses, donkeys and oxen, which were trained
for carrying heavy goods and for transport. The Arabs bought papyrus
mats from the Dinka women to carry back to their homes in Muglad,
to thatch their dwellings. This was a seasonal trade. During peacetime
in this area the dry season was something both sides looked forward to.

Civil war has complicated relations between the Dinka as a whole,
not just the Ngok Dinka of Abyei, and the Baggara Arabs. Without
any regard to the community relationship that existed between the
Messiria Baggara Arabs and the Dinka, Khartoum opted to use the

Arabs in order to subjugate the South. The Baggara Arabs as a whole, not just the Messiria Arabs of Southern Kordofan, but also the Rezeigat Arabs of Southern Darfur, became instruments of repression against the Dinka during the long wars of liberation against Khartoum. They were armed and equipped to kill any Dinka on sight and to capture, loot and keep anything they could find in the Dinka country for themselves, including human beings as slaves. This may have been why there was a surge in slavery during the war of liberation.

All this, together with the horrendous atrocities that have been inflicted on the Dinka communities by the North, have made matters very difficult to resolve. But resolved they must be, because without resolution the Ngok Dinka of Abyei will not find peace in their ancestral land and may even lose their land permanently.

The skirmishes that continue to take place in the Abyei area of the Ngok Dinka have encouraged the Arabs to settle the Dinka land. These issues can only be worked out in peace, between the two states of Sudan, South and North, and not by any other intervention, including war. The Ngok Dinka of Abyei may feel that they are capable of resolving this conflict by force of arms, but clearly they need to reconsider. Their territory is not big enough to sustain a war across many generations. They also do not have the numbers for a long and engaged contest. The leaders of the Ngok Dinka community of Abyei in the SPLA do not have the free and independent backing of the South. It is a deception and a bluff to command the SPLA to go to war with the North over Abyei.

Ordinary people in South Sudan are fed up with war. They feel that the war of liberation has not been worth much to them, considering the pathetic way in which they have been administered during the last ten years and that some of the Abyei leaders of the SPLA have been part of this mismanagement. Those leaders need to step back and return to basics in order to see that the solution to the Abyei problem is clear. It is the Abyei protocol of the CPA, which Colonel Garang personally negotiated. The problem is that he met a very untimely death, and the leaders of the Ngok Dinka of the SPLA want to impose implementation of the protocol on the other parties, and this will not work. They need to step back and seek to implement the protocol peacefully and in cooperation with Khartoum. We have seen what all these international border commissions and The Hague arbitration tribunal are worth – nothing to the Ngok people. Let them pursue reconciliation and mutual respect with those who are their neighbours and will remain so for ever, the Messiria Baggara Arabs and the government in Khartoum. This also means that the people of Abyei themselves must admit that the conflict between themselves and the Messiria Baggara Arabs is a local one, between two neighbouring or territorially adjacent communities. The role of Khartoum and Juba is to cajole, persuade and to compel these two neighbours to live in peace, rather than in war.

The question of the common borders between the two tribes can be worked out. Once that is done and the Ngok Dinka are satisfied that their land remains intact, and the Messiria Baggara Arabs are satisfied that their means of livelihood – the seasonal grazing of their cattle at the River Kiir – is guaranteed, the two governments can then go back to implementing the Abyei protocol. This is a responsibility that they must carry out. The Ngok people of Abyei must have the final say under the protocol whether or not they want to remain as part of Northern Sudan or revert to the South.

One final mistake made by the Ngok Dinka leadership of the SPLM has to do with the unofficial referendum that was conducted at Abyei in 2013. As expected, this resulted in an overwhelming vote in favour of the Ngok Dinka people of Abyei returning to South Sudan. Unfortunately, because it was carried out without the normally accepted due process, neither the government of South Sudan in Juba nor the government of Sudan in Khartoum has recognized it. In what amounts to game playing, the Ngok leaders of the SPLM are continuing to call on the international community to recognize the result of this informal vote. Yet this is a non-starter that does not help the cause of the people of Abyei, nor show that the political leadership in Abyei today has a serious attitude.

The government of the young republic of South Sudan, in whose name these leaders of Ngok are on occasion causing havoc, has not seen fit to halt these damaging political games. If the Ngok Dinka people of Abyei were capable of imposing their solution on anyone, they would have done so already, before the current leaders of Abyei came onto the political scene. As it is, the unofficial referendum has not worked. It has only complicated the search for a real solution.

Just the other day, as I was working on this book, I saw an appeal – an outcry, really – which was made by the local chief of the Ngok Dinka of Abyei to the international community. Chief Bulabek Deng Majok Kuol Arop said, in a tearful voice, that his community has been let down, abandoned by international players. But was the international community ever really engaged with the Abyei situation? The facts appear to be to the contrary. What has happened so far is that the political leaders of Abyei in the SPLM have assumed so much power for themselves that those who are in a position to bring the Abyei situation to the attention of the international community have sat back and are watching the Abyei leaders play their game.

When the chief made his tearful appeal, one can only hope that he knew about the process of international intervention on behalf of any people around the world. The international community has so many institutions and institutional procedures in place elsewhere that one must doubt whether a small and localized situation such as Abyei will ever gain its attention. Clearly, the chief must have been misled by the repeated bravado of Deng Majok Kuol Arop's children, the leaders of the SPLM, about how they make the world tick. And perhaps he should have learnt from the result of the arbitration case at The Hague.

The games that have been played by SPLM politicians, which mislead responsible people such as Chief Bulabek Deng Majok Deng Kuol, are not confined to the leaders of the SPLM from Abyei. This is an ongoing problem with the leadership of the SPLM in general. Although this attitude might have worked very well while the war of liberation was going on, it is about time that these leaders are realistic about what propaganda stories to tell their people.

The chief of the Ngok Dinka people of Abyei had been made to believe that the Abyei case would go to the highest forum in the world and would be resolved. If such a contention is put into the mind of an important individual such as the chief, then what can stop him from thinking that a solution to the predicament of his suffering people is possible?

Traditionally, the chief's family has always sought compromise with the Messiria Baggara Arabs. The SPLM leaders have now introduced a misleading notion that the problem of the Dinka Ngok people of Abyei can be resolved without the need to seek cooperation and compromise with the Arabs. This is a political fallacy – and a tragedy for Abyei's cause.

In order for the international community to become involved in this situation, there must first be a process through which an international intervention can take place. It is at present difficult to imagine, even if international statutes are invoked, that the necessary steps would then be taken to reach the level of an international intervention. At the head of any international intervention around the globe is the United Nations. The UN has its own executive body called the Security Council, which is the main body that can decide on an action. The route to a UN Security Council action is a rather difficult one. The Security Council has fifteen seating members at any one time, and five of these fifteen members have a veto vote on any issue that comes before them. A veto vote can simply put an end to any action by the UN Security Council.

Furthermore, the international community is organized into national governments, such as the government of Northern Sudan to which Abyei belongs as a territory and the government of South Sudan, to which most Ngok people of Abyei may have a desire to revert. This means that any international intervention in the case is already a contentious matter between Khartoum and Juba. Surely it is much easier and simpler to resolve the contention between them as neighbours rather than dragging it into the international arena?

Before a regional or a domestic problem such as Abyei goes to the UN it must first be dealt with regionally. Each world region has its regional political organizations: for example, there is an African regional organization called the Organization of African Unity (OAU). For Abyei and the people of both Northern Sudan and South Sudan, there is a sub-regional organization of which both countries are members – the Intergovernmental Authority on Development (IGAD). If Chief Bulabek Deng Majok Kuol Arop wants the international community to intervene on behalf of his people, set out here are the procedures through which such an international intervention may take place. I know, however, that this is not how Deng Alor Kuol Arop and Luka Biong Deng Majok Kuol Arop want the Ngok people of Abyei to understand the process of international intervention – these gentlemen behave towards their people as if they can simply order an international intervention and it takes place.

The international community will be involved with the Abyei situation only when Khartoum and Juba are involved in the search for a resolution – and only if Khartoum and Juba say that they have disagreed on how to resolve the Abyei situation to such an extent that they need international intervention. This is how these things work. It is not when local representatives think they are big enough, or powerful enough, to call on the international community to intervene and the world will come running. Leaders mislead themselves and their own people when they assume powers that they do not possess.

The presence of a UN force in Abyei may be misleading the people of Ngok, who think their leaders brought this force to Abyei. The truth of the matter is that the peacekeeping force was in Sudan before the South voted for its independence in 2011. It is part of a peacekeeping force to ensure that the CPA, the peace agreement that ended the civil war between the South and the North, is properly implemented. When the implementation of that peace agreement seemed to falter in Abyei, the UN deployed it to ensure that the security of the people of Abyei was safeguarded while the parties to the CPA sorted themselves out. It is not a force for either conflicting party – South or North – to use against the other.

Khartoum and Juba need to find a way to get along with one another in order to implement the Abyei protocol. Any part of the CPA that is not properly implemented will not go away. There is no deadline on any part of it. This is an agreement that has attempted, in text at least, to regulate relations between the people of South Sudan and the people of Northern Sudan, and needs to be implemented in full, including demarcation of the borders between the two countries. Without proper implementation, in full, relations between South Sudan and Northern Sudan will not become normal. The sooner the governments in Juba and Khartoum understand this and make the representatives of the people of Abyei and the Messiria Baggara Arabs understand this too, the better it will be for peace.

Resource and Wealth Complications

The politics of Sudan and the relations between South Sudan and Northern Sudan have always been complicated by wealth and resources. And so it is now in the Abyei situation. We have already seen how water and cattle grazing forced the Messiria Baggara Arabs to claim the Ngok Dinka land as their own. If they had had no need for grazing and watering during the dry season, they might not have had the need to claim someone else's land. This is not something that Sudanese ethnic communities normally do, because each community knows their land. This is the traditional way, even though, of course, the Arab tribes are the last immigrants to Sudan and have been taking land from its owners.

If a land is being fought over, no matter how long the war lasts it cannot be said to belong to those who have pushed away the owners of the disputed land and claimed it as theirs. In this, the wisdom of the ruling Ngok family of Arop Biong is borne out by the claims that the Messiria Baggara Arabs are making over the Ngok Dinka land. When Chief Arop Biong decided in 1905 to allow the land of the Ngok Dinka of Abyei to be administered by the British colonial authority as part of Kordofan in Northern Sudan, perhaps he wisely foretold what was to follow. Clearly, the Baggara Arabs had already been seasonally migrating to the Ngok Dinka country. It might have been much more difficult to regulate and to contain them if the seasonal migration had been resisted.

The Arabs were encroaching on foreign land with impunity. Rather than risk hostility from them, Arop Biong, his son and his grandson decided that it was better to be part of Kordofan so that the Baggara Arabs would feel that during the dry season they were moving into a land from which they were not restricted, and that the chief who permitted them to enter the Dinka land, Arop Biong, was also their chief. This seems to have worked out well for quite some time, until hostilities between the political North and the political South became part of the equation in the relationship between the Arabs and the Dinka on both sides of the political divide.

Now, given that Sudan is now two countries, South and North, and the border Dinka community of Abyei want to return to the now independent South Sudan, the parameters have drastically changed. We must recognize the reason why the Messiria Baggara Arabs are making claims to convert the Dinka land into an Arab land. This is a situation that requires very careful treatment – even the hot-headed leaders of the SPLM from Ngok cannot easily ask their people, or indeed the entire people of South Sudan, to go and reclaim their land by force.

The availability of new wealth in the Ngok Dinka country has complicated the matter even further. In reporting the dispute over Abyei the world media has perhaps exaggerated the situation – referring to the 'oil rich' area of Abyei. I have already talked about the dispute over Panthou (Heglig) – and how much the oil discovery in Abyei has complicated the situation is already clear. How this circle can be squared must remain an important question. So far, the easiest and cheapest way for the leaders of both South Sudan and Sudan to deal with the Abyei situation is seen to be the gun. But it is also clear to any sensible human being that the gun is not the solution. The leaders need to think again, and to think very hard indeed.

It seems obvious that the leaders of South Sudan and Northern Sudan should bear in mind that whatever solutions they find, sharing resources between the people on both sides of the border is the best way forward. If this is not guaranteed, the denied side is not going to allow the side with the wealth to enjoy that wealth in peace. And how many international peacekeeping forces are the two Sudans prepared to have deployed in their countries to prevent them from continuing the war with each other?

Chapter 4

Shared Responsibility between
Juba and Khartoum

One of the reasons why the political, the security and the economic situations in both South Sudan and the Republic of Sudan have so deteriorated is that both sides have refused to accept that they share responsibility for what they have done to their countries and people. The CPA – when it was negotiated in Navaisha, Kenya, and signed by the two warring parties of Sudan, the National Congress Party (NCP) regime in Khartoum and the SPLM in South Sudan – was a peace agreement designed for both parties to accept shared responsibility. From day one of its implementation, however, the entire six years of the interim period has been spent on the blame game.

Khartoum was not ready to spend energy and effort on implementing any development project that might have persuaded the people of South Sudan to postpone their vote on independence, to persuade the South to stay in unity with the North. The Northern Sudanese, having convinced themselves since independence in January 1956, indeed before that, that South Sudan had nowhere to go but to remain an undeveloped property of the North, the North did not want power sharing with the South. With the oil wealth from the South as its responsibility, Khartoum could have begun serious development projects in South Sudan, including in education, health and roads. Even if such projects could not have been completed by the time the referendum on self-determination was due, Khartoum could have requested a postponement in order to finish them. It would have been likely that even the SPLM, which had demonstrated its unreasonableness since the early days of the implementation of the CPA, may have agreed to this. These projects would have been the basis upon which the North could have been judged by the South as it voted on self-determination. Yet the North was so sure that the South was not going anywhere that it was happy for the South to take the vote.

Just imagine that if in January 2011 South Sudan had voted to remain in a united Sudan. Northern Sudan would have said, in my opinion, 'There you are, we've given you the chance to go, if that was what you wanted, and you haven't taken up that chance. Don't bother us any more.' A vote for unity would have been a vote for the North to subjugate the South even more than it had already during the nearly sixty years of independence. But the truth was that the South Sudanese could not stay with the North, knowing what they knew. It was better to brave the unknown. After all, that unknown was in the hands of their own children, the SPLM, who had fought for more than twenty-one years to liberate them from the North. The unknown could not possibly be worse.

The tragedy of the Ngok Dinka people of Abyei is that those who have been responsible for handling the Abyei case have continued to make mistakes for which they have refused to take responsibility. As a result, the people have almost totally lost a voice putting across their own case. Their leaders have decided that they have endless power; that they can influence the world community to come to their aid. While they seek to bring world influence to bear, the Abyei people lose hope and despair for a solution.

After Chief Deng Majok Kuol Arop defied all advice to return his people to South Sudan and to seek a peaceful border resolution, Abyei was soon caught up in the South–North conflict, a conflict that had its own political contradictions but was also compounded by the mistakes of its own political leadership. It was impossible, even without the complication of Abyei, to know where and when the case of South Sudan would be resolved. For sure, the ordinary Ngok people could not have guessed that the South would secede from the North. How could they, when the history of South Sudan itself ranged from unity, without even seeking autonomy – the view of the unity party of Santino Deng Teng – from the early 1950s to the mid-1960s; to the regional autonomy of the 1972 Addis Ababa Peace Agreement; to fighting for a united Sudan under the SPLM.

When a political movement or leadership representing any people anywhere in the world does not clearly define the cause for which they are fighting, it becomes confusing to subject the cause to conjecture. If the Ngok Dinka people of Abyei had only been deciding whether or not to revert to South Sudan or stay part of Northern Sudan a solution might have been possible many years ago, even long before the larger conflict between Northern Sudan and South Sudan was resolved. Unfortunately, as this chapter will show, crafty and unruly political leaders have developed amongst the Ngok Dinka people of Abyei. These crafty and unruly political leaders who have used the cause to curry influence in Khartoum and the bush of South Sudan in equal measure during the war and in power in Juba, without any regard to the real facts of the case.

When the Anya-Nya war of liberation for South Sudan first started in the mid-1950s, it was not clearly defined as a war of liberation. At first it was an uprising for jobs rather than a fight for a separate country. This is why it was possible to settle that war in March 1972 with an offer of regional autonomy by Khartoum to the South. Clearly, if Khartoum had respected its part of that agreement, Sudan might never have broken up again in 2011. The South was happy to stay in a united Sudan after the 1972 agreement, and to enjoy its small portion of self-rule, even though the South had no constitutional powers, because the agreement had offered the Southern leaders jobs.

Because they were happy with the 1972 agreement, most South Sudanese political activists, especially those who led the Anya-Nya movement, wanted to be in Juba to enjoy the fruits of the agreement in the South amongst their own people, rather than facing the perpetual political struggle between the South and the North in Khartoum. The Addis Ababa Peace Agreement could have been a final settlement with the North if Nimeiri had not become greedy.

When some Ngok intellectual political activists wanted the Abyei case revisited, because Addis Ababa had hinted about a possible referendum on the subject, the North acted in a rather heavy-handed manner, detaining them in Khartoum without the South raising any objection. The Ngok activists could not be allowed to tamper with the autonomy of the South. They were freed only after a peaceful intervention by

one of their own, Francis Mading Deng Majok Kuol Arop, who was a
member of the regime in Khartoum and friendly with its leadership,
rather than by political intervention from the South. What happened
to the Abyei activists in the late 1970s and early 1980s was a clear
indication that the Abyei case was not going to be easy to resolve with
Khartoum. It is hard to see why the political activists and leaders of
Abyei today are not able to recognize this fact.

After the 1952 Abyei Conference, in which Chief Deng Majok
Kuol and his followers refused to allow the British colonial powers
of Sudan to return Abyei to the South, most South Sudanese felt that
Abyei was not a political cause for which they would take up arms if a
political resolution could not be found. Unfortunately, the leadership
of South Sudan is not frank about this; and the Ngok political leadership is not realistic about what the South can and cannot do for the
Abyei cause.

Then came the real muddling and confusion that the SPLM liberation policy inflicted on the cause of the Ngok people. As close allies
and confidants of the late liberation leader of South Sudan, Colonel
Garang, the leaders of Abyei seemed quite happy that the South was
now fighting for a 'New Sudan', a united Sudan, in which it did not
matter where one's people were. This is in spite of the fact that it was
clear the idea for an independent South Sudan always came through
in the liberation debate. Unfortunately, in that debate, only the voice
of the leader, Colonel Garang, really counted. And only that one voice
seemed to matter to the leaders of Abyei within the SPLM.

Colonel Garang was a political realist. He never ruled out any option
as long as it did not divide his movement. He was also a crafty leader.
When it became clear that it was not only South Sudanese who did not
believe in the liberation of the whole of Sudan, in order to create a 'New
Sudan', he took almost a year to negotiate the 2005 CPA with which to
end the twenty-one-year civil war. He enshrined the right of the people
of South Sudan to self-determination in that 2005 peace agreement.

Nor did Colonel Garang let down the people of Abyei and the other
people of the Northern Sudanese regions who joined the SPLA and
fought with him for the liberation of and the creation of 'New Sudan'.
In the 2005 CPA he successfully negotiated the two CPA protocols,

one for Abyei and the other for the people of the Nuba Mountains of Southern Kordofan and the Angesina people of Southern Blue Nile.

Unfortunately, Colonel Garang lost his life in July 2005, just as he had begun to embark on the implementation of the CPA with Khartoum. Had he lived, the chances are that the people of Abyei would have had their referendum and would have voted to return their people to South Sudan. The CPA protocol for the Nuba Mountains and the Angesina Hills would also have been carried out.

What afflicted the implementation of the two CPA protocols needs to be traced back to the mistakes of the living, rather than to the late Colonel Garang. Unfortunately, these mistakes continue to be made and the people of these three regions of Northern Sudan continue to suffer in equal measure.

The Southern Kordofan and the Southern Blue Nile protocol clearly calls for a popular consultation amongst the peoples of these two regions to decide on what type of self-rule they would prefer in their relationship to Khartoum, the leader of the two regions having decided, even while the war between them and Khartoum was raging, that they wanted to remain part of a united Sudan.

Because there was already perpetual disagreement between the parties of the CPA, and because popular consultations were preceded by gubernatorial elections, the fight became one for power between the two parties to the peace agreement, rather than cooperation. Had the two parties of the CPA cooperated during the six years in which they were supposed to implement the protocol, the situation that now prevails in the two marginalized regions of Northern Sudan might have been avoided.

The leaders of the Nuba Mountains and the Angesina Hills did not want to wait for the final outcome of the popular consultations amongst their people. Instead, they wanted power for themselves there and then. If there was going to be popular consultation with their population, as indicated in the protocol, that process could only be conducted under their authority. As always, the SPLM leadership knew it all. No one stood back to consider what the regime in Khartoum had in mind.

Khartoum was, of course, calculating how to outsmart the SPLM leaders in the two marginalized regions of Northern Sudan. The ruling

NCP decided it would take one governorship of the two disputed regions of Northern Sudan and give one governorship to the SPLM-North. Once Khartoum had made the decision to share the two governorships with their peace partner, the SPLM, it was not important to them how this decision would be carried out. After all, it was Khartoum, not the SPLM, that was fully in control of these two marginalized regions.

Khartoum decided to allow Malik Agar of the Angesina Hills to win the governor's seat for that region. He was, after all, the leader of the SPLM-North, and if that movement had to continue to talk to Khartoum during the period that remained of the six-year interim period of the CPA, it was better to be able to talk to the leader of the SPLM-North.

As to the governorship of Southern Kordofan, the seat of power for the Nuba Mountains people, Khartoum decided it had to keep this position at all costs. The area is close to Darfur, where Khartoum still had problems. This area could not be lost to another rebellion. Like the Southern Blue Nile governorship, the candidate for governor of Southern Kordofan was the leader of the SPLM-North in the Nuba Mountains, Abdel Aziz Adam el-Helhillu. He lost to one of the National Islamic Front's best political operatives, Judge Mohamed Harroun. Once again, not calculating the possibility of their success before acting, the SPLM-North ordered its army, the SPLA-North, to contest the election result by force of arms. The result is that at the time of writing Khartoum controls the state government of the Nuba Mountain state at Kadugli, the capital, while at the same time the entire countryside has been devastated as a result of the war that was triggered in the SPLM-North's quest for the governorship.

It is impossible to predict what Khartoum might have done if the SPLM-North had pursued popular consultations amongst their people in the two marginalized regions of Northern Sudan instead of the governorship. But because the CPA is an internationally witnessed document, whose implementation is also being observed internationally, the chances are that Khartoum would have complied with the type of self-rule that the populations of these two regions indicated. And if the two regions had indicated a particular system of self-rule, this had to be acceptable to Khartoum, because that is what the CPA calls for.

Thus it seems natural that the SPLM-North would have assumed power in these two regions, whether Khartoum liked it or not.

As it is now, the political ineptitude of the SPLM-North leadership has returned the two regions to a devastating war, which the SPLM political leadership is not able to help. Indeed, all the leaders of the SPLM-North are now either refugees or, worse, political exiles.

For the Abyei protocol, which calls for a clear-cut referendum by the Abyei people, the matter has been complicated by the intransigence and arrogance of those who are in charge. While mismanaging the implementation of the Abyei protocol, the Ngok leaders of the SPLM, who thought of themselves and no one else as the inheritors of Colonel Garang's power, have also began to mess up the terms of cooperation over the implementation of the CPA between Khartoum and Juba. This is because they thought they had limitless power to do whatever they wanted.

For those who are responsible for the security and welfare of people, the first thing they should think about is how the decisions they take will affect the people. This has not been so with those responsible for the affairs of the people of Abyei.

The Messiria Baggara Arabs who make claim to the Ngok Dinka territory are clearly holding Khartoum hostage when it comes to the land issue between the two countries, because they do not want the Ngok Dinka land to become part of South Sudan, even though they know that the South will not deny them the privilege to graze and water their livestock in the Dinka country during the dry season. The Arabs know the big difference between a privilege and a right. Privilege can be withdrawn if the circumstances under which it was granted change, whereas rights cannot be withdrawn. Hence their ridiculous claim that the Ngok Dinka land of Abyei belongs to the Baggara Arabs. They maintain that it was because of their generosity that they invited the Ngok Dinka to settle Baggara Arab land. Perhaps, therefore, we should establish once and for all who first settled the land.

One of the facts that did not arise throughout the discussion of the land in Sudan has been that the Nilotic communities of South Sudan were always here – or at least from before records began. If anything, they occupied the banks of the River Nile up north, to the borders with

Egypt, long before Arabs set foot there. Through the Arab invasion, conquest and settlement along the Nile, the Nilotic nationalities were pushed further south, finally settling much of the present land along the River Nile and many of its tributaries. This means the Ngok Dinka of Abyei had settled the land long before the Messiria Baggara Arabs arrived. The Arabs' claim for the Ngok Dinka land cannot, therefore, be backed up by any facts.

Of course, the nature of traditional land conquest is that anyone who has conquered land from another people and has settled on that land for an appreciable period of time is entitled to claim the land for themselves. That is why much of Northern Sudan, especially along the banks of both the White and Blue Nile Rivers, is now Arab territories. But for the Messiria Baggara Arabs to claim that the Ngok Dinka territory of Abyei is a Baggara Arab land is taking things too far. This, of course, is not the same thing as saying that the Abyei territory does not belong administratively to Kordofan, and therefore is not part of Northern Sudan. Like the Baggara Arabs themselves, there are many South Sudanese who argue that because the Ngok Dinka territory of Abyei belongs to the Ngok Dinka, it must therefore belong to South Sudan – Bahr el Ghazal. This, again, is another wild claim, because geographical boundaries are not necessarily defined by ethnicity, but by administrative orders.

If ethnicity is the basis for land ownership, international law would not have prohibited ethnic cleansing. All the political systems of the world would have had to cleanse territories before they were named – and might they have all been named after the nationalities that cleansed them?

The real political ethnic and social case of the Ngok Dinka of Abyei, who claim they want to be part of South Sudan, is not just that they want to join their larger ethnic community, which largely constitutes the states immediately south of the Ngok. The real reason is that this people chose freely (at least their leaders did) some hundred or so years ago to be part of Northern Sudan. But they have not been accepted nor treated very well by their Baggara neighbours to the North. It is only fair that the leaderships of the two Sudans, North and South, find a peaceful way to allow this to happen.

As has already been stated here, the Abyei protocol of the CPA is part of the political agreement between these two neighbouring countries and needs to be fully implemented. As long as both Sudans recognize that the CPA ended a civil war between them that neither of them was capable of winning outright, the leaderships should have the common sense to carry out all the CPA protocols and normalize relations between the two countries in order to ensure a more durable, if not a permanent, peace.

One of the failures of both governments has been the fact that they have tried in a most unreasonable manner to rehash the issues that they failed to solve during the long civil war. If such an attitude is not replaced with truly genuine and honest mutual respect, then the Abyei problem will not be resolved and the tension between the two countries will become a way of life for both sides. That cannot resolve the Abyei problem.

One of the saddest failures of leadership, which continues to prevent any forward move over the Abyei issue, is the role played by the Ngok leadership of the SPLM in South Sudan. This is a leadership that has arrogated to itself the right to use the power of the government of South Sudan to prevent the resolution of the Abyei problem. With the Abyei protocol of the CPA worded the way it is, only by mutual consensus between Khartoum and Juba can the protocol be implemented. Taking this into account, the three young leaders, all from the ruling family of Deng Majok Kuol Arop, must take total responsibility for preventing the SPLM ruling leadership of South Sudan from normalizing relations with Khartoum.

Deng Alor Kuol, for instance, was in two very crucial key positions in Khartoum during the six years when the CPA was being implemented. He started off as minister for cabinet affairs. One of his famous statements when he was in this position was to publicly declare that a policy that had been announced by President Omer Hassan Ahmed el Bashir, the president of the republic, who signed the CPA with the South and appointed Deng Alor Kuol to his position in the cabinet, was not government policy.

In one of the reshuffles, Deng Alor Kuol was moved from minister for cabinet affairs to minister of foreign affairs. Both positions belonged to the SPLM during the six-year interim period. As minister of foreign affairs, he was even more ridiculous. Not only did he become an obstructionist, refusing to implement any foreign policy of a still united Sudan, but he debased himself by becoming a courier, carrying messages from European foreign governments to President el Bashir, rather than vice versa. These messages sought the demise of the president he was supposed to be serving as foreign minister. Deng Alor Kuol urged his president to surrender to the International Criminal Court (ICC), which had indicted him, not for the many crimes Bashir's government committed against the South during the civil war, but for crimes committed in Darfur, part of Northern Sudan from which South Sudan was about to secede.

While the CPA was being negotiated in Kenya between the central government of Sudan in Khartoum and the SPLA, another civil conflict in Sudan erupted in the country's western region of Darfur. The international peace mediators in Kenya had to press on with the configuration of the peace agreement between the South and Khartoum in order to bring an end to one conflict that had already had a horrendous impact on the population of South Sudan, rather than lump that issue in with what was beginning to occur in Darfur.

In due course President el Bashir was indicted by the ICC in The Hague for what was going on in Darfur, but this had nothing to do with the implementation of the CPA in the South. Deng Alor Kuol was in the interim government of Sudan under President el Bashir, because of the peace agreement with the South. If he wanted to take the moral high ground in Sudanese politics over what was taking place in Darfur, since he was in el Bashir's government as a representative of the South, he should have declined his position in the government, rather than ridiculing the cause of South Sudan by becoming a foreign agent and foreign courier.

I, of course, was part of the implementation of the CPA, as an adviser to the presidency of the Republic of Sudan in Khartoum. My personal view about the indictment of President el Bashir by the ICC was that many millions of South Sudanese had died at the hands of General el Bashir's army during the twenty-one-year civil war with the South. The ICC was already established when the long bloody civil war was raging in South Sudan, with its many casualties. More than three million died. The representatives of the people of South Sudan in General el Bashir's government could not give up the implementation of their peace with el Bashir because of Darfur.

President el Bashir had the sense to recognize that the only way to end the war in the South was to sign the peace agreement, which we were implementing with the support of the international community. To indict and arrest a man who had ended such a bloody civil war and was implementing a peace – and to indict him because of a second civil war – was to say that lives that were being lost in Darfur were more precious than those that were being saved in South Sudan through the implementation of the CPA.

When I made this point in the media at the time, I came to learn that Deng Alor Kuol had agreed with Luis Moreno Ocampo, the ICC prosecutor, to threaten me with indictment myself, because of what I said in defence of President el Bashir. In one of his reports on el Bashir's case to the UN Security Council, Mr Ocampo called me an obstructionist of the international criminal justice system.

In the end, Deng Alor Kuol could not fit into a government of national unity, supposedly set up to implement the CPA. Since he was one of the individuals who had dominated the SPLM leadership as one of the so-called John Garang boys, and could pick and choose government positions as he desired, he decided to leave Khartoum and return to Juba, where the Garang boys dominated not only the government but also the policy towards Khartoum. He chose for himself the juicy portfolio of the minister for cabinet affairs – in effect, becoming the serving prime minister of the South – and dominated the decision-making process of the young government of South Sudan, a political system in which each minister was in fact a president, because he was appointed by a president who had forfeited control over his government. Eventually, he plotted with others to overthrow the elected president and government of South Sudan by force of arms on 15 December 2013. Even today, Deng Alor Kuol has once again entered that government in Juba in the name of the so-called peace, in order to continue his political games.

When an individual feels he has all the power in his hands, there is nothing that he feels he cannot do. So it was with Deng Alor Kuol and the gang of his cousins and friends from Abyei. No constraints and the feeling of being ever-powerful had led to the leaders of Abyei within the SPLM machine in South Sudan feeling that every power was theirs. They acted with impunity across the board. Some of their actions were not only costly, but also totally unnecessary.

As mentioned already, these costly actions included three or four times attempting to take over the small territory of Abyei by force of arms. Lieutenant General Pieng Deng Kuol, one of the five top commanders of the SPLA, failed on each occasion. Even a non-military thinker and planner might have tried this once, but learnt from the act. To do it twice, or three, or four times simply tells you that the sons of Deng Majok Kuol Arop, who now find themselves with a free political hand in South Sudan, are a very dangerous group of people, even to their own Ngok Dinka community of Abyei.

In these kinds of war games, being played out over Abyei, very many innocent non-Ngok South Sudanese have lost their lives. This is at a time when the legitimate power of South Sudan has not made the decision that capturing Abyei through the use of the South Sudan army is in the best interests both of the people of South Sudan and the people of Abyei.

For anyone who knows Abyei as a territory, and knows the intricate interests that must be balanced there, it is clear that in order to arrive at a lasting peace agreement that would be acceptable to all sides one must rule out the use of military force. A real peace must be arrived at, and the only way to do this is to hold the two governments in Juba and Khartoum accountable to the terms of the Abyei protocol and to ensure, through proper observation and discipline, that it is implemented.

In the last reshuffle of the military and political leadership of the SPLA, General Pieng Deng Kuol became chief of the national police of South Sudan. It is never stated in the South Sudanese system of government why changes like this are made. But if the idea was to move him away from the army, to ease the confrontation with Khartoum over Abyei, because he was always visiting Abyei with a mighty military force, then nothing has changed. In the SPLM system, the military and the police are equally potent forces. However, at the time of writing, Lieutenant General Pieng Deng Kuol had been removed from his new post. It would appear that some political upheaval has afflicted the Deng Majok Kuol Arop family within the SPLM political establishment as a result of their dubious role in the attempted coup in Juba on 15 December 2015, which attempted to overthrow the elected government.

When I visited my Twic Mayardit community area, which is adjacent to Abyei, during the 2015 Easter holiday, Pieng Deng Kuol was there too, visiting Abyei with a powerful police force that was stronger than any military force that I had previously seen him with in the area. A show of force like this by Deng Majok Kuol Arop's children of the SPLM is that they make a resolution to the Abyei problem through the Abyei protocol impossible to achieve.

The Abyei protocol is part of the peace agreement between South Sudan and Northern Sudan. It is not an agreement between the Abyei people and Northern Sudan – there is no such agreement. The outcome of a referendum by the Abyei people will eventually become a commitment by Khartoum to respect the wish of the Ngok people of Abyei, if that wish be that they want to return to South Sudan. For now, however, when Khartoum sees these characters taking power in the South in the way they have done since 2005, Khartoum only sees Juba preparing for war over Abyei, rather than seeking peace. It is difficult to understand why, even if they have the power of South Sudan in their grip, these children of Deng Majok Kuol Arop, for the future of their own people and land, do not want to sit back and allow the legitimate leadership of South Sudan to negotiate the final peace that may return the Ngok people of Abyei to the South.

The third and the last of Deng Majok Kuol Arop's children I mentioned in the earlier part of this chapter, and who also plays a role in the misuse of the power of South Sudan in the name of the people of Abyei, is Luka Biong Deng Majok Kuol Arop. As part of the powerful gang from Abyei, he was a powerful player in the name of South Sudan in the relationship between Khartoum and Juba, a relationship that has now come to serious loggerheads.

At the outset, just as the implementation of the CPA began, Luka Biong Deng Kuol was minister for presidential affairs of South Sudan.

Because the president of the government of South Sudan was also the
first vice-president of the Republic of Sudan during the interim period,
Luka Biong Deng Kuol had the opportunity to work for a cooperative
relationship between Khartoum and Juba that could have facilitated
the smooth implementation of the Abyei protocol. Unfortunately, these
Abyei boys did not see that the CPA could be smoothly implemented
through cooperation with Khartoum. Instead, their idea was to use the
CPA to undermine Khartoum, in order to bring about regime change.
The result was that Juba succeeded in alienating Khartoum and all
sections of the CPA, including the Abyei protocol, remained unimple-
mented for six years. Now, relations between Juba and Khartoum are
virtually a state of war. It is anyone's guess as to whether the implementation of the Abyei protocol will ever take place.

Luka Biong Deng Kuol was also at one time part of the central
government of national unity of Sudan in Khartoum. He was at one
point minister for cabinet affairs. His worst misuse of power in Juba was
not necessarily related to not reaching an agreement with Khartoum,
but had to do with how he used the presidential power of the young
state of South Sudan to divide its people. This young political zealot
may have read the colonial saying 'Divide and Rule' and might have
seen himself as a new colonial ruler. However, there is a saying in Juba
that is quoted by many South Sudanese, that the Ngok people of Abyei
say they are in Juba to run the country for the South, because they are
better educated!

If Luka Biong Deng Kuol did not like you or did not like your
group, you had no right in South Sudan as an individual or as a group.
The outcome of this policy was that entire sections of South Sudanese
society were excluded from participation, no matter what their role had
been in the liberation struggle of South Sudan.

My own Twic Mayardit section of Warrap state of South Sudan
had to endure much pain at the hands of these young power wielders
from Abyei. Twic Mayardit is, of course, the closest to Abyei in terms
of geography and proximity. If you need to run away from any area of
Abyei southwards, you cannot avoid Twic. The region is a life-saver for
the Ngok Dinka people of Abyei, and Twic has never let them down.
Even while this gang of Deng Majok Kuol Arop's children was causing

havoc among the Twic community, the leadership still clearly saw that if there is any space for these people of Ngok it will have to be in the Twic Mayardit community. It is a source of personal pride to me that there is a society in South Sudan that still has a vision for the future of its neighbours.

I was a personal witness of the bloody civil war during which all the societies of South Sudan had to fend for themselves in order to survive. The Ngok Dinka of Abyei, having been displaced by the Messiria Baggara Arabs and the regime in Khartoum, had all run into Twic. The Twic community, with the leadership of their local SPLA commanders, organized themselves not just to survive but to resist the Baggara Arab onslaught, on behalf of the Khartoum regime.

Seven food-drop air strips were prepared by the Twic community to take advantage of the UN relief programme under Operation Lifeline Sudan (OLS). John Mangok Kuot, a brilliant workaholic young SPLA officer from Twic, appointed by Justin Yac Arop, the SPLA relief and rehabilitation director in Nairobi as the local SPLA relief officer in Twic, had a brilliant relief agenda for the Twic community. He inspired the Ngok people to set up their own air-drop field, which he added to the other seven strips for Twic, all of which were used by the United UN OLS to air-drop food supplies to the Ngok community.

John Mangok Kuot did not confine the Ngok community of Abyei to their own air-drop spot; he also included them in the distribution of food from the seven other air strips all over Twic. This was because, fleeing from Abyei, the Ngok Dinka had travelled long distances from their homes and had to be supplied from there.

Both John Mangok Kuot and Justin Yac Arop were amongst the leaders of the SPLA Twic community who died in a plane crash in 2009 as they were flying back to Juba from Kuajok, the capital of Warrap state, after attending a local SPLM conference.

When I visited Twic Mayardit to attend a local community conference at Easter 2016, I was confronted with many local problems caused by their Ngok Dinka of Abyei neighbours. These are not necessarily new problems, but have been exacerbated by the uncouth behaviour of the local Ngok Dinka administrators, who seem to take advantage of the current food shortage in Twic in order to pressure the Twic community over several issues. First, the Ngok community, currently resident on the border area with Twic, is attempting to encroach on what is well-established traditional Twic Mayardit territory and is calling it Ngok land. It will not be the first time that such claims have been made between neighbours – the problem has to do with how those in charge of administration on both sides handle the situation and deal with it.

The feeling in Twic is that when the Ngok are under pressure from the Messiria Baggara Arabs, the entire Twic Mayardit community responds very positively and very quickly to support and assist them. But when the Twic Mayardit community has a problem, the Ngok people of Abyei take advantage of that, and even use it to place pressure on Twic. Two very telling examples occurred recently which demonstrate this attitude of the Ngok Dinka people of Abyei towards their Twic neighbours.

At the time of writing, the Twic Mayardit community, indeed the entire Bahr el Ghazal, if not the entire South Sudan, is facing food insecurity. The problem is the same for the Ngok Dinka people of Abyei, because rains failed in 2015 across the whole South and the harvest was poor; but Northern Sudan had a good harvest in the type of foods that the North usually shares with the South as a staple – such as sorghum (dura). Northern Sudan had a bumper harvest of dura for two years in succession and some skilful traders from the North opened markets in a place in Abyei called Noong, one of the traditional homes of Chief Deng Majok Kuol Arop. There is a big market there, just a few miles north of the currently UN-occupied Abyei town. Members of the Twic Mayardit community go to Noong to buy food for their families. They reported to me when I was in Twic in April 2016 that they are being mistreated and exploited both by the Ngok community and by the local administration for Abyei, which was set up and is funded by the government of South Sudan.

I heard from someone who bought at Noong a container of grain that will not last a family of three for a month for more than 2,500 South Sudanese pounds, approximately US$50. The new administration of Abyei then taxed this grain exorbitantly, so the Twic Mayardit family had to pay US$25 for only US$50's worth of grain. And to whom do these heavy taxes go?

The Twic Mayardit community is, of course, bitter because the administration of the Dinka Ngok at Aneet is not only appointed by the government in Juba, but also that Aneet is a Twic Mayardit territory. The Twic Mayardit allowed the Ngok community to settle there during the war because they were fleeing from the Messiria Baggara Arabs unleashed on them by the government in Khartoum. Now, Aneet is a town, of a sort, for the Ngok, and is being used against its traditional owners.

The retired Catholic bishop of El Obeid, Macram Max Gassis, has set up a Catholic Church centre in Aneet, with a primary school for the children of Ngok and Twic in the vicinity. It is said that the Twic children are not permitted to attend this school. Another complaint of the Twic community is that the Ethiopian contingent of the peacekeeping force for Abyei is mistreating the Twic civilian population.

When all these problems were raised to me at Ajak Kuac, the administrative county headquarters for Kuac Madut Ring, my own section of Twic, all that I could tell the huge crowd was to be patient. Yet how long the patience of a people who feel continuously aggrieved can last is not easy to say.

When the war of liberation for South Sudan was going on, many of the displaced Ngok people of Abyei were allowed by the Twic community to settle in the border areas between the two sections as a temporary measure. Now, the Ngok leadership administering these Twic community areas have included the areas that are clearly Twic areas in Abyei territory. This creates unnecessary problems. For people struggling to keep their own traditional territory from the encroachment of the Messiria Baggara Arabs, the current leaders of the Ngok people should know better. And how does it help the Ngok people to be known as troublemakers with their neighbours both North and South?

Unfortunately, without knowing the facts of this situation, the contingent of the Ethiopian army now keeping peace in the Abyei area has drawn borders between the Twic and the Ngok, even though they have no way of knowing whose land it is. What is clear is that the Ethiopians ought not to involve themselves in such local disputes when they are supposed to be peacekeepers.

Repeated reports from the area speak of the local Ngok leaders of Abyei reporting the local Twic people to the UN African force and asking the UN Ethiopian contingent to evict the Twic communities from their own land. I fail to appreciate how the Ngok Dinka people of Abyei can square continuing to fight for their own land from the Arabs, with the support of their neighbours in South Sudan, yet at the same time encroaching on the areas of people whose support they will always need.

Power grabbing by the Ngok leaders of the SPLM is not only confined to the local neighbours of Abyei in Twic; it extends far into South Sudan itself. When he was minister for the presidency of the Republic of South Sudan, Luka Biong Deng Kuol was repeatedly quoted as saying that the Ngok had succeeded in marginalizing the Twic community from the political power of South Sudan, and that 'The Twic are finished'. Being out of the government of South Sudan now, he may deny such utterances, as he has denied other utterances quoted elsewhere in this work that he made at the time when he was breathing his greatest power. But very serious damage has been done and needs repairing.

Grabbing power for the ambitious young leaders of the SPLM from Abyei has had no limits. There have been complaints from everywhere in South Sudan. The political misbehaviour of Deng Majok Kuol Arop's children within the SPLM is reminiscent only of the behaviour of the Northern Sudanese merchant class when Khartoum controlled the South after Sudan gained its independence on 1 January 1956. The Northern Sudanese traders in the South not only became the principal advisers to the Northern Sudanese rulers of the South, but they also occupied the South's parliamentary seats and therefore became the representatives of South Sudan in the so-called national parliament in Khartoum. Fortunately, Deng Alor Kuol Arop could not get away with this type of political game, and had to give the parliamentary seat of Tonj district of Warrap back to its rightful owners.

Tonj was an area of South Sudan that ought not to have been belittled by outsiders posing as political enlighteners of the local community, which is what Deng Alor tried to do. As a political community, Tonj is one of the more enlightened of the Dinka communities of South Sudan, more so than Abyei. During colonial times, as the British began to permit some semblance of enlightenment for the South Sudanese population, Tonj town became a well-renowned centre of education. It had a government primary school, a village school, a teacher training centre and one of a very few junior secondary school intermediate schools. Some of Chief Deng Majok Kuol Arop's children, renowned as political thinkers and scholars of the Abyei community – Francis Mading Deng Majok and Zacharia Bol Deng Majok Kuol – are amongst Tonj's scholastic products. Both were admitted to Rumbek Secondary School, the only South Sudanese secondary school at the time, before their father took them to Khor Tagat Secondary in El Obeid, in Northern Sudan. This was no doubt an attempt to enhance his political influence in Northern Sudan.

Tonj also produced some of South Sudan's renowned political leaders. William Deng Nhial, a distinguished public administrator before joining politics, defected from his public service post as assistant district commissioner of Yei district of Western Equatoria and joined the Anya-Nya liberation movement in the early 1960s. William Deng and Joseph Oduho jointly wrote the first ever book on the political cause of South Sudan. In the mid-1960s, after the overthrow of the first military regime in Sudan under General Ibrahim Abboud, William Deng returned to Sudan and organized an internal wing of the then Sudan African National Union (SANU), calling for a federal arrangement between the South and Northern Sudan.

The North threw out the federation at the March 1965 Round Table Conference, and massacred William Deng and his entire party entourage during the June 1968 elections in South Sudan. He had won his Tonj parliamentary seat in those elections as well as eleven other seats for his SANU party, intending to pursue his call for federation inside the Sudanese parliament in Khartoum. The power elite of Northern Sudan did not like even the idea of federation and so they murdered him.

The Tonj area that Deng Alor Kuol wanted to represent by proxy inside the SPLM establishment in South Sudan also had Dominic Muorwel Malou, one of the 1957 members of parliament from South Sudan in Khartoum, who had pressed the Northern Sudanese political elite for dishonouring their 19 December 1955 promise of a federation to the South. This promise was a deception aimed at deluding the South

Sudanese members of parliament to vote for the independence of Sudan. When this was proclaimed on 1 January 1956 and the South Sudan members of parliament wanted the North to deliver on its promise, the South was told that federation had been found not to be suitable for Sudan. Political power was handed over to General Ibrahim Abboud in a bloodless military coup on 17 November 1957. MP Dominic Muorwel Malou from Tonj and many of his colleagues from South Sudan had no choice but to join the Anya-Nya liberation movement in order to pursue political liberation of South Sudan. It was an act of total political naivety that Deng Alor Kuol could accept to represent by proxy from Abyei a district of South Sudan such as Tonj.

Political representation is not something you can assign in South Sudan without serious consideration. This is not the United States of America, or Europe, where a political party can transplant a candidate in an electoral constituency into an area from which that candidate does not come. These types of practices do not work in South Sudan, even though the SPLM, Deng Alor's ruling party of South Sudan, pretends that it can make it work.

Deng Alor Kuol had to be forced by the local people of the Tonj electoral consistency to vacate their seat to make way for their own local representative. That is also why, no matter how loud a noise Edward Dut Lino Wuor Abyei may make that he represents the Abyei, the Abyei people will never allow him to represent their interest anywhere, because he simply is not one of them.

The Hague Gimmick

From the stories so far recounted in this book, it must be clear that the catastrophe for South Sudan was the extreme exercise of power by the SPLM leaders who are running South Sudan, who believe they have limitless strength that they can use without any restraint. Volumes can and will certainly be written in the future about their misuse of power during the period when they ran South Sudan after losing their leader, Colonel John Garang, at the onset of the implementation of the CPA in 2005. Overusing power that they did not have in the first place makes it difficult to resolve problems such as the implementation of the Abyei protocol.

Amongst these problems, as previously mentioned, is taking the case of Abyei to the International Court of Arbitration at The Hague. They knew this was not going to work; it was merely an attempt to embarrass Khartoum, because Khartoum was already under pressure by the Western powers who wanted a regime change. All the shenanigans of the SPLM leadership failed, though. It is clear that if they had succeeded it would have meant the end of the CPA, as no party or individual in Northern Sudan, besides those who signed the CPA in 2005, wanted it. To each and every Northern Sudanese who was not a National Islamic Front (NIF) member, signing had been treason. Fortunately for the South, the CPA was not successfully undermined from within the South itself.

Going to The Hague for international arbitration cost South Sudan dearly in terms of border demarcation. Without much thought, Deng Majok Kuol Arop's sons were aiming to enlarge Abyei as a geographical territory; and this is what continues to happen as the borders between the Ngok and Twic Mayardit are tampered with.

Taking the Abyei case to The Hague was a show of power and also an attempt to embezzle some wealth from the South. Was it necessary to send so many Ngok leaders to The Hague to testify? How much did it cost South Sudan? No one in South Sudan was accountable to anybody else concerning how South Sudan's money was spent.

In the South Sudan media, the Abyei area was presented as 'oil rich', implying that this was why Khartoum did not want Abyei to go to South Sudan. But at this time, Khartoum was still controlling the entire oil industry in South Sudan. If the idea was to sit on South Sudan's wealth, Khartoum would not have complied with the referendum on self-determination in the South and would not have recognized the independence of the South from the North. But in fact the vote on self-determination in 2010 facilitated the independence of South Sudan with the full cooperation of the North. If the North had not cooperated, the referendum would not have taken place. We are seeing clearly in Darfur what happens when Khartoum is not willing to cooperate with the international community.

So what did the arbitration decision from The Hague achieve? The Abyei leaders of the SPLM claimed that Panthou, a well-known village of the Panaru Dinka section of Western Upper Nile, which Khartoum had annexed to Kordofan like Abyei, was part of the Ngok Dinka of Abyei territory. This was a pathetic act of greediness; there was no evidence for this. Khartoum had renamed Panthou with the Arabic name Heglig – merely translating the Dinka name for a particular wild fruit tree. Heglig has no common border with Abyei and is far away from the area. For the Ngok leaders of the SPLM to claim Heglig, because it has oil, like Abyei, was a blunder that has cost South Sudan dearly.

The International Court of Arbitration, after considering the evidence presented by the Ngok leaders of the SPLM, ruled that Heglig belonged to the North and not to Abyei. It is difficult to understand why the court ruled that Heglig belonged to the North, rather than merely ruling that it did not belong to Abyei. South Sudan and the Panaru Dinka people now have to wait for another, hopefully fairer, arbitration to return their area of Panthou to them, whether or not Heglig continues to produce oil.

Land is, of course, paramount, whether there is mineral wealth there or not.

In the meantime, the Ngok leaders of the SPLM continue to commit blunder after blunder as they attempt to break the Abyei impasse. Everyone involved ought to know by now that the Abyei case is a difficult case that cannot be settled by use of force. But can anyone persuade the Abyei leaders of the SPLM to see sense? It seems that this possibility is still far away, as long as the sons of Deng Majok Kuol Arop within the SPLM continue to believe they are able to impose a solution on Khartoum by force.

The Illegitimate Vote

The latest blunder by the leaders of Ngok within the SPLM was conducting a poll in Abyei. There was no proper procedure for the conduct of that referendum – no laws followed, no registration of voters, no monitoring, nothing – and the result was unsurprisingly overwhelmingly in favour of the Ngok people of Abyei returning to the South. When a plebiscite is conducted properly the vote may still go that way, of course, but it has to have a legal basis. Fortunately for the people of Abyei, this referendum has not been affected the stance of Juba or Khartoum, both of whom have not recognized this farce of a referendum and still seem committed to holding a proper Abyei referendum under the CPA.

All these mistakes by the Ngok leaders of the SPLM have made the resolution of the Abyei problem much more difficult. And they still believe that only they can make South Sudan governable.

Consumed by power and material greed, they have entangled themselves in the political conflict within South Sudan itself. Deng Alor Kuol Arop has been accused of being one of the military coup leaders who attempted to overthrow by force the first elected government of South Sudan under President Salva Kiir Mayardit in December 2013. Deng Alor Kuol and his group were detained, only being released thanks to the intervention of President Huhuru Kenyatta of Kenya. The bitterness which that blunder created in South Sudan means that no one within the SPLM mainstream, or indeed in Juba and Khartoum generally, is even thinking of Abyei as a conflict area now.

Because of Deng Alor Kuol's actions and because the relationship between Juba and Khartoum was so bad to begin with, Khartoum is now working with the South Sudanese opposition led by Riek Machar Teny, who directed the failed December 2013 military coup attempt in Juba. Deng Alor Kuol and those who support him in Abyei, such as Edward Dut Lino Wuor Abyei, have joined Riek Machar in an effort to overthrow the legitimately elected government of South Sudan. This means that the Abyei problem will have to wait until this internal conflict is resolved.

In the meantime, the government in Khartoum is happy to play the spoiling card in the South by supporting the rebel Riek Machar Teny, since no love is lost between Juba and Khartoum. How long this entangled web of hate between Khartoum and Juba will last is anyone's guess.

Fearing his own life because of these misdeeds, Deng Alor Kuol and his group have now returned to the fold of political power in Juba. This has been thanks to the efforts of many others. The peace process now being undertaken by IGAD has so far failed to produce any tangible results; if it succeeds, the beneficiaries are the supporters of Riek Machar Teny and Lam Akol.

Riek Machar Teny thought that the gang of SPLM spoilers, now known as eleven former political prisoners, would join him as political subordinates whom he would then spoonfeed with scraps from his share of power if there is ever a peace agreement between himself and the government in Juba. It now seems that this is not going to happen, even as part of the new South Sudan peace agreement.

Since the gang of eleven former prisoners had no military force to display at the peace talks, even the IGAD peace mediators, who seem to suggest a type of peace in South Sudan that has never been tried anywhere before, impose a leadership that has no guns to silence on the peace process.

The only other possible involvement of these former political prisoners from the SPLM leadership should have been through the type of political reconciliation that the ruling party of Tanzania has been brokering in Arusha, Tanzania. President Salva Kiir Mayardit seems to accept this Tanzanian initiative. It seems clear that in the interest of peace in South Sudan, President Salva Kiir Mayardit would accept any peace initiative from anybody. But at first these former political detainees wanted Juba to implement the Arusha plan in their absence from Juba, before they returned home. This is a matter of security, as far as they are concerned. Appointing them to their former positions in Juba may be the only security guarantee that will persuade them to return to Juba.

These eleven are very senior military and political leaders of the SPLM. They know how their army, the SPLA, behaves when matters like the events of December 2013 go badly wrong. They cannot return to Juba without first ensuring that both their political positions and their guards are in place. With matters not so straightforward in South Sudan, it could prove a long wait. This means that resolving the Abyei protocol will also wait for some time. The Ngok leaders of the SPLM have entangled themselves in a sad web of political blunders that has stalled the implementation of the protocol.

Perhaps time is not of the essence for a problem that has already lasted more than a hundred years. What is important is that in the end the people of Abyei are able to decide. Only in this way will there be a resolution of the Abyei issue.

Unfortunately, it is impossible to advise the Ngok leadership of the SPLM, because they think they know it all. The question is not really what advice they will take, but whether other SPLM leaders from other parts of South Sudan will take responsibility for the mistakes they have made and begin to correct them.

First, the leaders of the SPLM must recognize that Abyei is not a conflict issue between them and Khartoum, in much the same way as the problem of the marginalized people of Northern Sudan, the Nuba Mountains of Southern Kordofan and the Angesina people of Southern Blue Nile, is not a problem between Khartoum and Juba.

The people of these three regions – the Nuba Mountains, the Angesina Hills and Abyei – joined hands with the long-struggling people of South Sudan, who had been fighting for their own right of self-determination from the North since 1947, when the British colonial powers decided the two parts of the country had to be treated and administered as one country. When the South demanded to be treated separately from the North at the 1947 Juba conference, the leadership of both the Nuba Mountains and the Angesina Hills did not raise any questions about their own status. Indeed, in fairness to the people and leadership of these two marginalized regions of Northern Sudan, they have always wanted to be part of a united Sudan. Throughout the war of liberation by the people of South Sudan, which these two regions joined, the idea, definitely rejected by the South, was to fight for a united Sudan – a Sudan that would end marginalization and give black African stock of Sudanese descent a stronger hand over the Arab stock that had dominated the country and to whom colonialism had handed over power when Sudan attained its independence in January 1956.

While the leader of the South Sudan liberation struggle, Colonel Garang, had been a unionist of sorts, preferring to liberate the whole Sudan and to rule it, being South Sudanese he understood and accepted the strong feelings for self-determination in South Sudan. Garang did not let down any of the four groups, including the Ngok people of Abyei.

As the principal negotiator of the final peace between central government in Khartoum and South Sudan, Colonel Garang accorded every one of the four groups their dues. He negotiated and signed a deal with Khartoum that allowed the people of the Nuba Mountains and of the Angesina Hills each to conduct popular consultations to decide the type of self-rule the people wanted. Colonel Garang also negotiated a deal for the Ngok Dinka people of Abyei, allowing them to exercise a plebiscite in which they would decide either to remain in the North or revert to South Sudan.

It is, perhaps, because of the death of Colonel Garang in July 2005, just as he was starting the implementation of the CPA all over Sudan, as the first South Sudanese first vice-president of the Republic of Sudan and the leader of the totally autonomous South Sudan, that the two Sudans are in the mess which they are in today. A strong leader who was beyond reproach, Colonel Garang would have ensured that popular consultations were conducted in Southern Kordofan and Southern Blue Nile and that the results of these consultations would have been implemented. The Abyei plebiscite would also have been conducted, and the results respected.

With Colonel Garang off the scene, the SPLM leaders of the Nuba Mountains converted the wishes of the people into a quest for political power for themselves. Seeking power for the individual leaders over the political views of their populations has thrown the two regions into the conflict that now engulfs both of them.

The results of the 2010 elections in both Southern Blue Nile and Southern Kordofan were not conclusive. The leader of the Angesina Hills people, Malik Agar, won the governorship of that state, with an apparent corroboration of Khartoum. The leader of the SPLM in Southern Kordofan, Abdel Adam Aziz el-Helhillu, lost to the candidate of the NCP, the ruling party in Khartoum, Ahmed Haroun. El-Helhillu did not accept the result and decided to use force to take over the capital of Southern Kordofan, Kadugli. He failed. The result is a war that still rages at the time of writing. That war has devastated the entire Nuba Mountains region. This is typical of the SPLM leadership's behaviour.

Anyone other than the SPLM might have weighed all the options carefully, and should have allowed popular consultation of the people to take place, which would certainly have resulted in some sort of regional self-rule and would have forced the imported NCP governor to hand power to the local leadership and return to wherever he came from. As it is now, the people of the Nuba Mountains have no political say in how they are being administered by Khartoum, which still runs the region, because popular consultations have not yet been conducted. The people have as yet made no political decision about how they should be administered. This is what the popular consultation is supposed to give them.

To overplay issues is very typical of the regime in Khartoum. There is now war between the leaders of the SPLM-North, who purport to represent the people. Because of the military skirmishes that followed the 2010 elections, there are no direct lines of communication between the regime in Khartoum and the SPLM-North political leadership. All the leaders of these two Northern Sudanese marginalized regions have been accused by Khartoum of having committed atrocities and have been sentenced to death in absentia. But the real mistake has been that the leaders of the SPLM-North are now part of the political struggle in Khartoum for a regime change. Unfortunately, if there is a regime change, there is no guarantee that whoever takes power will give autonomy to the three marginalized regions of the North, including Abyei.

The African Union (AU) mediating team, led by the former president of South Africa, Thabo Mbeki, continues to try to hold meetings between the two sides elsewhere in Africa, but does not seem to be making any headway. After more than thirty years of trying to impose a military solution or defeat the regime in Khartoum outright, it is incredible that the SPLM leadership continues to believe that only war with Khartoum will settle matters. There does not appear to be any concern for the perpetual suffering of the ordinary citizen, who craves some respite and peace.

Because the relationship between the two governments in Khartoum and Juba has not been normalized since South Sudan became independent in July 2011, Khartoum has now found itself fanning the conflict in South Sudan. The story in Khartoum is that the perpetual rebel of South Sudan, Riek Machar Teny, has pledged that if he succeeds in overthrowing the elected independent government of South Sudan he will unilaterally declare the reunification of South Sudan with Northern Sudan. Clearly, this is something Khartoum cannot give credence to.

The leaders of Sudan know that Riek Machar Teny cannot overthrow the independent government of South Sudan, let alone unilaterally declare unity with Khartoum. Even those fighting with him against the government in Juba cannot go along with him. What he is doing – which Khartoum is fanning – is tribal warfare.

Riek Machar Teny falsely claims that he is leading his Nuer tribal white army against the Dinka government of Salva Kiir Mayardit in Juba. This is far-fetched. The Nuer community has its own leadership that will not be lured into falsehood. Unfortunately, Khartoum has its own agenda and feels that it has the chance to destabilize South Sudan on the cheap. Give a handful of peanuts to Riek Machar Teny and you will maintain the instability of South Sudan.

For a long time, Khartoum has been accusing Juba of supporting the many rebellions that are afflicting Sudan. Both sides deny these claims. The truth is in a grey area between the two. There is at least some public evidence for Khartoum's standpoint. At one point, in 2014, the chief of Sudanese national security, General Mohamed el Atta, declared in a televised statement in Khartoum, also shown in Juba, that they would support Riek Machar Teny until he took over power in Juba. At that point, it seemed to them that the forces of Riek Machar Teny were stronger than the forces of the South Sudanese government. Even if that was the case, this was an unfortunate mis-speaking by the Sudanese security chief. Clearly, attitudes like this make it much more difficult to imagine a resolution to the Abyei issue.

Back to Abyei and South Sudan, the government in Juba must now make it clear to the SPLM leadership from Abyei that it does not regard itself at war with Khartoum and that it considers that the Abyei issue comes down to implementing the Abyei protocol. Neither Juba or Khartoum can and should escape their responsibility to conduct the referendum. If this is not conducted, then both governments will have failed in implementing the CPA, a political document that has enabled South Sudan to become an independent country. The fulfilment of this responsibility requires the normalization of relations between Khartoum and Juba, and this will not be achieved as long as Khartoum believes that the Abyei sons of Deng Majok Kuol Arop in the government of South Sudan are continuing to dominate the decision-making process over Abyei. This is a matter of political give and take. Khartoum has come to the conclusion, rightly or wrongly, that all they are doing from the positions they hold in the government of South Sudan is to plan war against the North. The responsibility of the South Sudanese government is not to the individual members of the Ngok community within that government, but to the people of Abyei as a whole. The fulfilment of this responsibility is to carry out the referendum, even if this means laying off members of the Abyei community from the government of South Sudan, who have not assisted in the implementation of this noble goal on behalf of all the Ngok people of Abyei.

Chapter 5

What I Am Accused of Not Doing
for Abyei

Accusations against me by the children of the late Chief Deng Majok Kuol Arop in the ruling SPLM of South Sudan are not just multiple, but are unfounded. The reason I am recording these accusations in this book is not so that I can refute them, but merely because they need to be part of the story that I am relating here. Chapter 6 is an account of things I have tried to do for Abyei and its people whenever I have been in a role of public responsibility in Sudan, which I think will be sufficient rebuttal of the accusations against me.

Accusations against me by the SPLM leaders from Ngok started when I had some political disagreement with Colonel John Garang de Mabior, the late leader of the SPLM. The children of the late Chief Deng Majok Kuol Arop were amongst those closest to Colonel Garang at the time of my disagreement, and they must have thought it would enhance their closeness to the movement's leader if they were seen to take on his detractors. Besides this, apart from Commander Pieng Deng Majok Kuol Arop, none of them had any distinguished role of their own, so maligning me in public enhanced their own names in the liberation movement. The mouthpiece for this was the SPLM's radio station in Ethiopia, which had been nationalized by Colonel Mengistu Haile Mariam of Ethiopia from the Christian Church and handed over to the SPLM for political propaganda broadcasts.

Deng Alor Kuol in particular, who had been appointed by Colonel Garang to be the military governor of the SPLM in Bahr el Ghazal, my province, may have thought that he could enhance his own credentials with the liberation leader if he succeeded in tarnishing a known name in that community. Therefore, he made it his business to relate false-hoods in my name throughout the liberation period. It was put about that I was cooperating with Khartoum, and was against the cause of the Ngok people of Abyei. These stories by Deng Alor Kuol and his gang within the SPLM leadership in South Sudan continued to be recounted, even long after I had decided to step aside from active politics in South Sudan after the South voted for its independence in July 2011. I did not want my name to detract from the leadership of South Sudan. The liberation had been achieved, which is what I wanted, so I wanted to leave the running of South Sudan to those who said they had liberated the South on their own.

In Juba, in 2012, a meeting was convened in an attempt to reconcile the Ngok Dinka of Abyei and the Twic Mayardit community of Warrap state, my own community, who are neighbours. These two communi-ties had their own problems, which had nothing to do with me. I was not in Juba, and I had not been invited to attend the meeting. Several such meetings in Khartoum between these two communities before the South seceded from Sudan had come to nothing, and during them Deng Alor Kuol had continuously accused me of not wishing the Dinka Ngok people of Abyei to return to South Sudan. So attending these meetings was of no use as far as I was concerned.

I had my own political differences with Colonel Garang about the ultimate objectives of the liberation. This did not go beyond a differ-ence of opinion, but Colonel Garang's supporters took matters much further than their leader.

While it was true that in the liberation culture of the SPLM move-ment, contradicting the stated opinion of the leader was tantamount to a death sentence, the leader himself allowed some room for different points of view – especially if those views were being held by someone who was not a member of the movement, like me.

At some point Colonel Garang was irritated by some of my views that contradicted his public position, and he may have hinted to the children of Deng Majok Kuol Arop that it would be desirable to get rid of me – if they did it their way and it was not traceable back to him. Yet as far as I know, Colonel Garang did not directly ask any of Deng Majok Kuol's children to lynch me. Rather, these boys in the SPLM may have felt that if they did so it would have pleased the leader. Nevertheless, nothing came to pass. So I am still here, writing about these events.

I know, for instance, that after I established the *Sudan Democratic Gazette* in London, from 1990, and began to put out contrary opinion to the SPLM's stated objectives for the liberation, my differences with Colonel Garang came to a head and he made some effort to silence the paper and even to silence me. But when his efforts failed – because those he intended to take action on behalf of the movement did not want to be used for such a purpose and because the paper became a clear supporter of the liberation movement – Colonel Garang abandoned efforts to get rid of me. It was these early notions of political differences that misled many individuals within the movement to believe I had been an enemy of Colonel Garang.

Even the colonel's widow, Madame Nyandeng de Mabior, held a grudge against me because of my political differences of opinion with her husband. Some of these personal grudges continued even after Colonel Garang's death in 2005.

At the time of the helicopter crash that killed Colonel Garang, I was in the Lake District, in England, on a mountain-climbing holiday. I heard on the evening news that his plane was missing and was presumed to have crashed, but I received no further news. I decided to continue my holiday, as I had no role to play in the matter at all. The next day, when it became clear that the helicopter had crashed, killing everybody on board, Commander Salva Kiir Mayardit, having now assumed the leadership of the SPLM, telephoned me with the news.

Things usually work out in their own mysterious ways. Often, while high up on the hills in the Lake District, mobile telephones do not work. And even if they do, I switch my phone off when I am climbing, so as not to be distracted. But, on that day, I had not turned off my phone; perhaps subconsciously I was expecting someone to call me. After all, Colonel John Garang had been the leader of the liberation movement of my people.

Salva Kiir Mayardit had been second in command of the liberation movement for a long time. He had also been personally very close to me, and knew very well the little political irritants between the late leader and myself. He wanted me to be present at Colonel Garang's burial in Juba on 28 July. 'You cannot stay away from Garang's burial', he firmly told me. His tone of voice confirmed that I should do my best to attend as he requested.

Commander Salva Kiir Mayardit is someone very close to me. And, arguably, it is thanks to his vigilance that I owe my life, given the many shenanigans that the people around Colonel Garang threw up against me.

From 1998, when it became clear that Colonel Garang was not pleased with my political ideas and the way I was expressing them, my security and safety became a concern for all those close to me within the SPLM movement. Two individuals, Salva Kiir Mayardit and Justin Yac Arop, took it upon themselves to try to protect me whenever I was travelling in South Sudan, which was quite frequently during the war.

I was in regular direct contact with Justin Yac Arop, and it was clear to everyone who knew us that we were very close. He had been the executive director managing the SPLM office in Nairobi, and secretary for the Relief and Rehabilitation Office of the SPLM in Kenya. Whenever I planned to visit Kenya on my way to South Sudan, I always let him know. In his turn, he almost always immediately informed Commander Salva Kiir Mayardit.

As number two in the movement, Salva Kiir Mayardit was the number one person in charge of the war against Khartoum in South Sudan. He was an extremely busy man. Whenever Justin Yac Arop informed Salva Kiir Mayardit of the date of my arrival in Kenya, he almost immediately stopped whatever he was doing and came to Nairobi to meet me. He knew that I visited Kenya only when I was en route to South Sudan. During the civil war, all travel to South Sudan went via Nairobi to Lokichokio, where the UN's Operation Lifeline Sudan (OLS) was based.

Salva Kiir Mayardit and Justin Yac Arop travelled with me to South Sudan and stayed with me in the South until the end of every trip. We also returned to Kenya together, before they returned to their duties as SPLM leaders and I returned to the United Kingdom, which was my residence and base through the years of the Sudanese civil war, after I had left Khartoum after the military coup in June 1989, when General Omer Hassan Ahmed el Bashir suppressed my newspaper, the *Sudan Times*.

Salva Kiir Mayardit was the chief of security of the entire SPLM movement. He could not have based his personal protection of me on suspicion or hearsay. He decided to always be with me whenever I was travelling in South Sudan, in areas that were under the control of the SPLA, because he had clear evidence about the risks to my life. He definitely did not want to scare me away from my country, so he did not hint as to any suspicion he may have had.

As a movement, the SPLA had perfected ways of dealing with individuals like myself, who were perceived to be obstructionists of the policies pronounced by Colonel Garang. I assume that Colonel Garang had at some point aspired to silence me, not necessarily by killing me – although much of that was taking place in the SPLA – but at least by arresting and detaining me.

At least three of the former commissioners of Twic Mayardit county lost their jobs because they refused to carry out the order to arrest me. James Yol Kuol Bol was the first of these SPLM Twic commissioners to refuse Colonel Garang's orders to arrest me.

As commissioner of Twic, James Yol Kuol Bol was asked to report to Kampala, Uganda, for a special administration course. He had been a colleague of Colonel Garang during the Anya-Nya liberation movement of South Sudan during the 1970s and was senior to him in the movement. The two men knew each other well. While in Kampala, the Commissioner of Twic was invited to a special night with Colonel Garang at his home. He was informed that I was obstructing the movement's policies and that he should arrest me. James was told that he could count on the full protection of the movement if he took such a step. When he refused to obey he was immediately dismissed from his post as commissioner.

The same thing happened to the commissioner, who replaced him. Commissioner Aciei Akuen, an officer of the SPLA – a security officer at that – was ordered to arrest me for security reasons, but he also refused to comply and was fired.

A third commissioner of Twic, Awet Aken, had his own ordeal, quite different perhaps from those of the first two commissioners, but also for daring to have a good relationship with me. When he became commissioner of Twic, the CPA had already been signed by the SPLM on behalf of South Sudan and Khartoum, and its implementation had already commenced. The South had already set up an autonomous government to administer South Sudan over a six-year interim period before deciding on its future in a referendum. Twic Mayardit was still part of Warrap state (the country became twenty-eight states in 2015, with Twic Mayardit as a separate state). The governor of Warrap state at that point was a certain Bol Madut, someone who was entirely brainwashed with anti-Bona Malwal propaganda.

I became adviser to the presidency of the Sudanese republic in Khartoum during those six years. I inspired a road project that was being built by the central government of Sudan, from Heglig, in the Unity state of South Sudan, to Wau, the capital of Bahr el Ghazal. This new road passed through Twic county and included a new bridge that was constructed over the River Lol, at Wunrok Adiang, in Twic. Governor Bol Madut described this vital new communication line for South Sudan, linking an important oil depot at Heglig with Bahr el Ghazal, as Bona Malwal's road – and said that it was intended by me to facilitate an Arab invasion of South Sudan.

The governor refused to allow stones and gravel to be transported from Kuajok, the capital of Warrap state, to build the bridge at Wunrok, a distance of only fifty miles. In the end building materials had to be transported all the way from the Nuba Mountains, in Northern Sudan, to Twic, more than 200 miles, to build the road and the bridge.

When the road was completed, no Arab army from Northern Sudan ever attempted to use it to invade the South. On the contrary, it was Governor Bol Madut's own army, the SPLA, commanded by one of Chief Deng Majok Kuol Arop's sons, General Pieng Deng Majok Kuol Arop, who three times attempted to take over Abyei by force of arms from the North, using what had been nicknamed the Bona Malwal Madut Ring Road. All these attempts were futile and they all failed.

Before Bol Madut was appointed governor, I had been cooperating with his predecessor, Governor Anei Kuendit. I visited Turalei, the capital of Twic Mayardit county, from Khartoum without a problem, having normally informed the governor and Twic Commissioner Awet Aken of the dates of my visits. My route to Twic from Khartoum was via Heglig. I took a flight there from Khartoum and then travelled by helicopter to Turalei. All the information about these trips was given to the governor of Warrap state and the commissioner of Twic.

I normally visited Governor Anei Kuendit at his state headquarters at Kuajok, where he always cordially welcomed me without any problems. From Kuajok, I normally visited Wau, the capital of Western Bahr el Ghazal, where I have a home.

When Bol Madut became governor, he decided that I should not visit Twic Mayardit at all, even though it was the place of my birth. When I informed Commissioner Awet Aken that I was to visit Twic on a certain date and the commissioner in his turn informed the governor, the governor said I was not allowed to visit Twic. The commissioner requested Governor Bol Madut to put that order in writing, and he did so. In turn, Commissioner Awet Aken passed this on to me. I could easily have caused a row over Governor Bol Madut's behaviour. After all, the country was still one and I was part of the presidency of the republic. But I simply ignored him. I thanked the commissioner for informing me of the written order and told him I was going to my home anyway. I advised him not to implicate himself by receiving me, or even visiting me at my home once I arrived there. However, the commissioner refused to stay away, and therefore caused a problem for himself with his governor. When I arrived at my home, on the appointed day, Governor Bol Madut left the state, and took no further action against me. I was told later that the commissioner had become the scapegoat. The governor said that it was Awet Aken who had been confused, and that he had never written an order prohibiting me from visiting Twic. The poor commissioner was dismissed from his post. He remains one of my closest political supporters and confidants in Twic.

It was obvious that strange things were happening on the ground in South Sudan. There was a lot of talk that Colonel Garang's plane had been shot down by his enemies. As he had signed a peace agreement with Khartoum only a few months earlier and had just taken the oath of office as first vice-president of Sudan, Colonel Garang's enemies, who may have wished him out of power, had to be enemies from within South Sudan. As I was well known as one of his political detractors in South Sudan, I was obviously, to his close supporters, very much one of the late colonel's enemies from within. And this was merely because I spoke out, saying publicly that South Sudan was liberating itself from the North – not fighting to create a 'New Sudan', a united Sudan.

And so it transpired, when the body of Colonel Garang was laid to rest at what is now a famous mausoleum in Juba, and his entire family stood in line, led by his widow, Madame Nyandeng de Mabior and their children, beside the first vice-president of Sudan, Salva Kiir Mayardit, to receive condolences from the many heads of state who had come to attend the burial. At the head of the line of condolence receivers, Salva Kiir Mayardit shook my hand very solemnly, and with friendliness; Madame Nyandeng de Mabior was next in line. I extended my hand to her, but she refused to respond. Obviously, her children, who were next to her in the line, noticed this, and to avoid further embarrassment I proceeded without attempting to shake their hands. This was a lady whom I knew very well and who had previously been very polite and courteous to me, in spite of any political differences that I may have had with her husband.

For many years after the death of Colonel Garang the story continued to circulate within his circles in South Sudan that I was one of the people suspected of having had a hand in his death. The Abyei leaders of the SPLM, even though they had no evidence, became part of the group spreading this story.

It is incredible how a story like this could have gone on for so long. Northern Sudanese detractors of South Sudan have an Arabic description of the type of South Sudanese who perpetuate such incredible stories: '*Junubeen Massakeen*', 'Poor South Sudanese'.

At the height of the political differences between Colonel Garang and his number two, Commander Salva Kiir Mayardit, it was, again, the children of Chief Deng Majok Kuol Arop in the SPLA who caused havoc by fanning those differences. As an example, after Deng Alor Kuol failed to administer Bahr el Ghazal, to which he had been appointed by Colonel Garang – throughout his entire time in the liberation movement Deng Alor Kuol had shown no administrative ability whatsoever – the Ngok boys influenced Colonel Garang to transfer Commander Salva Kiir Mayardit there, as both the regional governor and the commander of the SPLA army. This was probably the first time that a liberation movement of any country transferred its deputy leader away from the centre of the movement's decision-making. There were two main reasons behind transferring Commander Salva Kiir Mayardit to Bahr el Ghazal at that point. First, it was almost certain to this group of Ngok boys within the SPLA that Salva Kiir Mayardit would fail, and hence would be humiliated.

By this time, Bahr el Ghazal was devastated by the war. Khartoum had armed both the Messiria and the Rezeigat Baggara Arabs of Southern Kordofan and Southern Darfur against the South, ordering them to destroy the entire Dinka community; to kill, loot and to destroy anything they could not take to the North with them. The Arabs excelled in this, to the extent that there was a surge in human slavery in South Sudan.

While I was publishing the *Sudan Times* newspaper, I featured stories about the Baggara Arabs' enslavement of Dinka women and children. In fact, the prime minister of the day, Al Sadig al Mahdi, inspired the Baggara Arab leaders to come to Khartoum to open a criminal case against me for making these accusations. All this, of course, was quickly put to an end when General Omer el Bashir seized power in the June 1989 military coup, overthrowing al Mahdi in the process.

By then I had left Khartoum and settled in exile in the United Kingdom. I established the *Sudan Democratic Gazette* monthly newsletter in London in 1990, and continued to publish stories about Arab slavery in South Sudan during the war.

The Swiss-based Christian Solidarity International (CSI) picked up on the enslavement of South Sudanese during the war. They raised funding around Europe and North America and started a slave redemption programme in South Sudan, in which they organized slave redemption trips to Bahr el Ghazal, and paid the Baggara Arab militia in Sudanese pounds to redeem the slaves. They then exchanged this slave redemption hard currency from US dollars into Sudanese pounds with the SPLA local commanders. On their part, the SPLA, now under the leadership of Salva Kiir Mayardit, used the funds to arm and supply themselves. In no time, the SPLA in Bahr el Ghazal managed to repulse any Arab militia attacks in Bahr el Ghazal and pacified the area. Politically and militarily, this was not good news for Colonel Garang and his clique.

Not to be deterred from their rumour-mongering and not appreciating any good done by Salva Kiir Mayardit to the community, Chief Deng Majok Kuol Arop's boys began hammering it into their leader that Commander Salva Kiir Mayardit had created a rebel army of his own in Bahr el Ghazal, with my support. They told Colonel Garang that the idea behind the strong organization of SPLA forces in Bahr el Ghazal was to stage a coup there, to topple the colonel and to hand over power and the leadership of the movement to me. Colonel Garang took the story so seriously that a strong schism developed between him and his number two.

This was probably the first time that Colonel Garang called in Salva Kiir Mayardit and demanded he distance himself from me, because I was not a member of the movement, nor a supporter of it. Salva Kiir refused to obey his commander-in-chief – because he knew I was a supporter of the SPLA, the South Sudan Liberation Army and more.

Deng Alor Kuol believes that it is because of Bona Malwal that Abyei has not been returned to the South from the North. This is because I say that Ngok will only return to South Sudan by mutual agreement between Khartoum and Juba, and not through any other means. Deng Alor Kuol and the other Abyei leaders within the SPLM believe that Abyei should be liberated through war. I do not agree with this, for the reasons that are given in this book.

The campaign against me was also a way in which Deng Majok Kuol Arop's boys could show they were the best protectors of the image of their leader. It is this group that created the idea that leaders should not be criticized, at least not in public. They went a little too far in saying that criticism of a revolutionary leader was a capital offence.

In the midst of such negative propaganda against me, my own relatives, friends and close political allies had often warned me about the personal risks I was running. Many of my friends did not want me to visit South Sudan during the war. I could not accept such advice and so continued my trips.

I had left Khartoum, where I had been living most of my adult life and where I had put out several publications – *The Vigilant* daily newspaper (1965–9) and the *Sudan Times*, also a daily newspaper (1986–9)

– that were critical of the regime of the day. It did not make sense that I should live abroad, publishing in London the monthly *Sudan Democratic Gazette*, which was actively supporting the liberation cause of my people, and yet be barred, or bar myself from visiting the country in which I had been born.

Of course, there were many individual members of my community who wanted me to be politically reconciled with Colonel Garang, so we could work together for the cause. One such was Francis Mading Deng Majok Kuol Arop, one of the more distinguished children of Chief Deng Majok Kuol Arop. Francis was close to Colonel Garang and frequently discussed my possible rapprochement with the leader of the South Sudan liberation movement.

As someone in the same age group as me, Francis had worked with me for a long time as a political ally. Francis always kept me posted on his conversations with Colonel Garang that were related to me. It was through the intercession of Francis and others that I eventually met Colonel Garang, and we worked out some way of understanding each other's approach.

As leader of the liberation movement of South Sudan, Colonel Garang had come up with the policy of liberating the whole of Sudan, which did not appeal to me. And because this 'New Sudan' idea did not appeal to many South Sudanese fighters under his command, he thought that it was the ideas of people like me that were preventing him from persuading them of the wisdom of his policy.

On their part, whether for opportunistic or genuine reasons, Deng Majok Kuol Arop's sons in the SPLM heartily embraced the 'New Sudan' idea. They were joined by the leaders of the Nuba Mountains and the Angesina Hills, all from Northern Sudan, who had all persuaded them-selves that there was no way for any black African in Sudan to break away from the Arab North Sudan. To these groups of black Northern Sudanese, 'New Sudan' was the only solution. In this context, ideas of individuals like me, who wanted to liberate South Sudan and sepa-rate it from the North, were not acceptable, and had to be condemned outright.

As the political cause of the Ngok Dinka people of Abyei could not be reconciled with the idea of a 'New Sudan', it appeared that the sons of Chief Deng Majok Kuol Arop in the SPLM had come to believe that Abyei would never be returned to South Sudan. Remaining in a united Sudan became, therefore, more acceptable to them than a separate South Sudan that left Abyei behind in Northern Sudan. Therefore, any expression of the right of the people of South Sudan to self-determination, by people like me, was unacceptable and had to be treated as a hateful and treasonable idea.

By 1994, the *Sudan Democratic Gazette* had established itself as a credible publication that supported the liberation of South Sudan. Colonel Garang had come to accept the paper as one of the publications that was promoting his cause. I did not often challenge the idea of the 'New Sudan' in the paper, although the political agenda of the publication had become well established. In my many conversations with Colonel Garang he had come to accept that self-determination did not rule out any other political steps. Since self-determination would be dependent on a vote among the people of South Sudan, this, to him, was a political idea he could work with. He felt that the people of South Sudan could be persuaded to vote for a 'New Sudan' instead of separation; that 'New Sudan' was a larger gain for the people of South Sudan than separation. Colonel Garang did not see how the people of the South would fail to embrace it.

During 1994 I managed to persuade my old friend Boutros Boutros-Ghali, secretary-general of the UN, to invite Colonel Garang to the UN in New York. The United States had initially refused to give Colonel Garang a visa to enter America and had accused him of being a communist, because of the support he was receiving for his movement from the communist regime of Mengistu Haile Mariam of Ethiopia.

After Colonel Garang had visited the UN, the Americans thought they should meet him too, to see if they could lure him away from Mengistu to do business with them. After all, the United States had been working for the demise of the Mengistu regime in Ethiopia. Since they had no particular problem with the cause of the people of South Sudan, which Colonel Garang was now orchestrating, why not deal with him? So from New York we went to Washington DC, where Colonel Garang had a very busy week, meeting all sorts of people.

In Washington another old friend, Assistant Secretary of State for African Affairs, Ambassador Herman Cohen, organized a meeting with Colonel Garang at his office at the State Department, to which I was also invited. This was the first public meeting I had ever attended together with Colonel Garang. It was all about the 'New Sudan' and how establishing it would be good for the people of Sudan, South and North. Clearly, the US diplomats at that first meeting with Colonel Garang were not satisfied with his political ideas. After all, the history of the struggle of the people of South Sudan against the North was a long one. How come the separatist South would now be happy fighting to create a 'New Sudan'? The Americans were silently asking themselves this question.

After this meeting, at which Colonel Garang put forward his theory of three intersecting circles (discussed in Chapter 3), we stayed in Washington for a few more days, after which Colonel Garang visited his old university state of Iowa. I returned to the United Kingdom. We never discussed his intersecting circles again, but the meeting did not affect our relations, which had vastly improved over time. It is true to say that we evolved a good working relationship after he finally convinced himself that I was not against his personal leadership.

This normalization of relations between me and Colonel John Garang de Mabier took some time to evolve. It finally came about after Colonel Garang came to believe that I was not one of the people behind the 1991 Nasir rebellion by two SPLA commanders, Riek Machar and Lam Akol. His internal clique, the Abyei boys and others, had convinced him that this was the case, in spite of the fact that I had denounced the rebellion on the pages of the *Sudan Democratic Gazette*, and in articles in other international media. The problem was that I had taken a message to Colonel Garang from Commander Lam Akol Ajawin a few months before the rebellion.

I had met Commander Lam Akol Ajawin at an African American Institute Conference in Cairo in March 1991. Lam Akol came to know that I was to visit Addis Ababa after the conference, and that I might get an opportunity to meet Colonel Garang, who was in Ethiopia. He pleaded with me to persuade Colonel Garang to convene a meeting of his high command. I did not want to know why he wanted this meeting.

Meetings are part of the natural course of any functioning system, and questions need not arise. All that I asked was whether or not I should mention his name to Colonel Garang. Lam Akol warned me not to, as the difficult relations between Colonel Garang and his commanders within the SPLA had become public knowledge, and no questions needed to be raised.

My meeting in Addis Ababa with Colonel Garang took place at, of all places, the residence of Deng Alor Kuol. I began by asking many questions about how the war was going. Finally, I asked about a meeting of the high command. This was at the point when he was telling me about many problems he was personally facing inside the movement.

When I told him that perhaps it was time he convened the meeting of his movement's high command, so that the other commanders could assist him with solving some of the problems, without the slightest hesitation, Colonel Garang said: 'Who wants the meeting of the high command? Is it not Lam Akol and Riek Machar?' I immediately told him that if the two senior members of his movement's high command wanted a meeting, then maybe he should give them a meeting.

This matter needed no further discussion, and so I did not try to persuade Colonel Garang. He sounded to me set against any meeting of the high command, and I really did not know enough about what was going on in the SPLA to persuade him otherwise. At the same time, I had made no commitment to Lam Akol about reporting back to him about my discussions with the colonel. Matters simply rested where they were.

For six months I met neither Lam Akol nor Colonel Garang again. Clearly, Lam Akol and his colleague, Riek Machar, must have got down to planning their August 1991 coup against the colonel. There was time enough for this. Perhaps Lam Akol's request to me in Cairo, to persuade Colonel Garang to convene a meeting of the high command, was a message to the colonel that was part of the coup signal.

Being a military man, Colonel Garang might have begun to be suspicious of me at that point. Nor do I doubt the fact that the colonel will have shared Lam Akol's message from me with his personal confidant, Deng Alor Kuol. The atrocities that followed the 1991 rebellion at Nasir against Colonel Garang were so horrendous that it is quite possible Deng Alor Kuol and his cronies within the SPLM decided to use those events to make mischief in my name.

The Nasir rebellion, like anything that happens within the SPLA, was used against the Dinka as a community, in the same way that the December 2013 rebellion in Juba, by Riek Machar, clearly supported by Deng Alor Kuol and Luka Biong Deng Majok Kuol, was also used against the Dinka. In 2013 the leader of the country was a Dinka, Salva Kiir Mayardit, and in 1991 the leader of the SPLA was also a Dinka, Colonel Garang.

In the 1991 rebellion, Deng Alor Kuol's immediate family paid a heavy price. At that point, the SPLA was very mixed. No one within the SPLA or outside it had calculated that there would be such a vicious rebellion in the middle of the national liberation struggle. Military coups are normally staged against the leaders of established governments, not within a rebel movement.

At Nasir, where Lam Akol and Riek Machar's rebellion was announced, there was a contingent of young Dinka Ngok SPLA army officers under the command of Riek Machar and Lam Akol. They were all massacred in a very gruesome way. Most of them were relatives of Deng Alor Kuol and the other clique of Deng Majok Kuol Arop's children, who are commanders of the SPLA. It was, perhaps, part of their maligning and tarnishing of my image for a long time that Colonel Garang and Deng Majok Kuol Arop's children kept on telling any South Sudanese who did not know the facts of the rebellion that I had been part of that horrendous rebellion against him.

Eventually, because of what I wrote at the time and continued to write about the rebellion, Colonel Garang came to realize that I could not have been a part of it. He eventually made amends with me on this and other matters. It did not matter to me, after that, if the Abyei clique continued to malign me about something I had nothing to do with.

Accusations and charges against me by the leaders of the SPLM have not ceased. The latest was by Deng Alor Kuol himself, in a meeting in Juba before he took part in the rebellion to overthrow the elected government of South Sudan. At what was supposed to be a reconciliation meeting between the Ngok Dinka of Abyei community and the Twic Mayardit community, my own community, he said I was continuing to deny the Ngok Dinka people their right to return to South Sudan. I was not at the meeting, but Deng Alor Kuol was responded to by others on my behalf.

Two important events in the series of accusations that were made against me are worthy of being recorded before I move on. In 1994, after the Umma Party of Sudan signed a political protocol with the SPLM, recognizing the right of South Sudan to self-determination, at Chukudum, in Eastern Equatoria of South Sudan, I sought to explain to the leaders of the Ngok Dinka of Abyei community in the SPLM why this was such an important political event.

Colonel Garang had authorized me and Peter Nyot Kok Malok, a distinguished South Sudanese law professor, who was also the representative of the SPLM in the Federal Republic of Germany, to prepare the document with the Umma Party. This was truly a milestone political move by the SPLM. Until this point, Northern Sudan had been united against the call for self-determination by the South. After the Umma Party signed with the SPLM at Chukudum, every Northern Sudanese political movement in Sudan came to accept that self-determination for the South was now the political bottom line in the search for peace in Sudan.

After the signing, I sought to meet the leaders of the Ngok Dinka of Abyei in the SPLM and to explain to them the background, not only to the Chukudum agreement, but also to the right of South Sudan to self-determination, which has nothing to do with whether or not Abyei will eventually revert to the South. I asked Deng Alor Kuol, who had witnessed the signing of the protocol between the SPLM and the Umma Party, to convene a meeting between me and the Ngok group. He obliged, arranging the meeting at his own residence in Nairobi. But as it transpired, Deng Alor and the other of Chief Deng Majok Kuol Arop's children in the SPLM plotted to use this meeting to insult me. Luka Biong Deng Majok Kuol Arop was designated to fire off the first abuse.

When the meeting convened, Deng Alor Kuol rightly assumed the chairmanship, since the meeting was in his house. I had no reason to suspect that there was anything afoot until Deng Alor Kuol called on Luka Biong to speak. When Deng Alor opened the meeting he immediately called on me to say what I wanted the Ngok community for. I went into some historical detail, explaining that the Ngok people of

Abyei have been part of Northern Sudan by their own choice since 1905; that the political relationship between the bulk of South Sudan and Northern Sudan needed sorting out; that the South had called for self-determination from the North since the Khartoum Round Table Conference of March 1965, because the North had refused since independence in 1956 to share power with the South in a united Sudan; that the Chukudum agreement, in which the Umma Party had just recognized the right of the South to self-determination, was an important landmark development. I concluded my presentation with a statement that we would have to adopt other ways of resolving the Abyei issue, rather than using it to slow down the political development of South Sudan. I was accompanied to this meeting at the house of Deng Alor Kuol in Nairobi, Kenya, by Ambrose Riny Thiik, who later became the first Chief Justice of the new Republic of South Sudan at independence in 2011. Because the meeting turned into abuse of me, and I had to end it quickly, Justice Ambrose Riny Thiik had no opportunity to talk and make his views known.

When I stopped speaking, Deng Alor Kuol called on Luka Biong to speak. He had not asked to speak, nor did Deng Alor Kuol look around to see if anyone else had his hand up. Without hesitation, Luka Biong took the floor and pointed his finger at me: 'You, Bona Malwal, I have documentary evidence to prove that you have sold away Abyei to Northern Sudan. Al Sadig al Mahdi has bought Abyei from you for the North. Al Sadig al Mahdi has promised you that you will be the first prime minister of Sudan from the South, if you let Abyei become part of the Messiria Baggara Arab land.' When Luka Biong ended his incredible antics, Deng Alor, again, did not ask anyone else to speak. He returned to me, and asked if I had anything to say in response.

It was now clear to me that I could spend the rest of the evening at Deng Alor Kuol's residence in Nairobi, Kenya, listening to this trash. I was leaving to return to the UK that same evening, and I preferred to spend what time was left to me before going to the airport doing other things. But before leaving Deng Alor Kuol's home, I took the floor and told Luka Biong and the Ngok members present that I came from a place in South Sudan; that I would not sell my own community.

After that evening I decided I would have nothing to do with the case of the Ngok Dinka people of Abyei any more. It has not been so easy to keep this promise to myself. There have been a number of political interventions concerning Abyei that I have taken part in. Since that meeting I have been to Abyei town at least once. I accompanied the body of that very distinguished educator of many South Sudanese, elderman and head teacher Lino Wuor Abyei, to Abyei from Khartoum, and took part in his burial there. Moreover, in Juba as well as at home in Twic, where I go at least twice a year, at Christmas and Easter, I meet many well-intentioned Ngok elders who know the closeness of my relations with their community, and want to discuss with me the plight of the Ngok Dinka people of Abyei.

In spite of the continuous presence of the children of Chief Deng Majok Kuol Arop in the political leadership of the independent government of South Sudan, Abyei remains a territory of Northern Sudan. It will not revert to South Sudan without a political agreement between Khartoum and Juba. Unfortunately, Deng Majok Kuol Arop's children continue to cause havoc in the politics of South Sudan, both inside the SPLM as the ruling political party and inside the government of South Sudan. At the time of this writing, Deng Alor Kuol has returned to the government of South Sudan as foreign minister. It is a political step that will help neither the South nor Abyei. Khartoum will perceive this as the government of South Sudan continuing to plan war with the North over Abyei.

The 2010 General Elections in South Sudan

Now I have to speak of the assault on me by General Pieng Deng Majok Kuol Arop of the SPLA. Pieng was one of the five chiefs of staff of the national army of South Sudan at that point. Most armies in the world do not involve themselves so blatantly in politics, especially in national election politics, but most armies, perhaps, are not as revolutionary as South Sudan's army. So General Pieng Deng Majok Kuol Arop arrogated to himself the duty to rig my electoral constituency in the 2010 general elections.

The president of the republic of South Sudan, Salva Kiir Mayardit, visited my constituency earlier in the election campaign. It was his duty, of course, to campaign for the SPLM candidates in the general election: he is, after all, the head of that political party. And the SPLM had promised itself that it had to rig every seat in the first elections in South Sudan after the war, to show the world that it was the most popular political party in the world. Most people in South Sudan almost certainly anticipated that the SPLA would do this.

When President Salva Kiir Mayardit visited my constituency during the 2010 general elections, however, it was a normal visit by a head of a political party in an election season. In fact, he was suspected by his own party of wishing to lose this particular seat to me, because of a long personal relation between us. He told the public rally that the SPLM had a candidate in the constituency and he wanted the community to elect him. He named his candidate and showed him to the public. Then came the remark that the SPLM brass suspected was tantamount to his endorsement of my candidature, instead of that of his own candidate. The president said the election was free, and that the electorate was free to elect the candidate of their own choice. The message was clear: the election should be free and fair. This was all that the electorate in my constituency wanted to hear from the head of the government of South Sudan. But, to General Pieng Deng Majok Kuol Arop and the cohorts of the SPLM, the president had given the seat away. And my defeat in those elections was a juicy one for the SPLM and needed to be ascertained.

General Pieng Deng Majok Kuol Arop took it upon himself as his duty to defeat me. But he knew there was no legitimate way of doing so. He and the SPLM leadership had to rig it. Besides President Salva Kiir Mayardit, the entire SPLM leadership was clear about this. This was a constituency that had elected me since 1968, when I first ran for that seat.

Elections in Sudan are, of course, not as regular as elsewhere, because of frequent military interventions in the politics of the country – with coups d'état that controlled the country for many long years without elections. But when there was a test of popularity in an election, even during a military dictatorship, and I ran, I won this seat. So it was not too difficult to predict what might have happened in the 2010 election if it was allowed to be free and fair.

The military regime of Jaafar Mohamed Nimeiri took power in Sudan only one year after I was first elected to parliament in Khartoum from the Twic North constituency in 1968. Nimeiri signed a peace agreement with South Sudan in March 1972. I became minister of information of Sudan in July 1972, as a result of that agreement. No elections took place in Sudan during the first six years of the Nimeiri military regime.

In 1975, the Nimeiri regime decided to subject itself to a popularity contest in an election. Although Nimeiri did not want his ministers to run, fearing that there could be a contest of popularity with him, something that no military dictator wants, I insisted that I needed to. Nimeiri was not happy, but there was very little he could do about it, except order me to resign my seat as minister before running. This was a far cry from the policy of a regime that had allowed civil servants to run in the election without resigning from their jobs. I was denied any election facilities, even those accorded to other candidates. Although Nimeiri eventually dropped the demand on me to resign as a minister before running for election, because I contested the legality of that position, I was denied any public facilities. My own legal right as a minister to use my government car was denied me, for example. Yet I refused to be distracted by a political squabble with Nimeiri.

The Nimeiri regime's electoral system lumped together large districts so that the election became a selection of the better-known candidates. In 1975, three districts were grouped together – my own district, Gogrial, with Tonj district, just south of Gogrial, and Wau district, west of Gogrial. These three districts had to elect five candidates to the parliament in Khartoum. This was a very difficult election. One would win one's seat only by topping the polls in all three districts. In many respects, it was a system that was anti-rigging.

Without knowing how it was going to work out, I decided that we needed to share out the five seats between the three districts. To me, it was a question of responsibility. Each of the three districts needed to be represented in parliament. Political party rivalry always rears its head, and so it did in this election – even though, in theory, this was a military regime era and General Nimeiri had dissolved all political parties when he staged his coup in May 1969.

In Bahr el Ghazal, my province, there had always been a contest between my party, the Southern Front, and William Deng Nhial's internal wing of the Sudan African National Union (SANU), which was leading the South Sudan liberation movement abroad at that time. William Deng had split away from SANU in exile and had returned to Sudan in 1965, following the overthrow of the first military regime of General Ibrahim Abboud. William Deng had been promised federation for the South by the North, which did not materialize. In spite of that, the internal wing of SANU because an internal political party inside Sudan, while the exile wing of SANU remained a liberation movement.

Bahr el Ghazal became the province of a political contest between the Southern Front and the internal wing of the breakaway SANU. I had to take charge of a team that I had put together as candidates in the 1975 election of cumulative constituencies.

My district, Gogrial, had registered electorates double the other two districts put together. Gogrial could have won all the five seats if that was what I wanted. I knew that in normal elections Gogrial was almost equal to Tonj. In the 1968 election, the first election that both our parties had contested, Gogrial had three seats and Tonj also had three. The Southern Front won all three seats for Gogrial. William Deng's internal wing of SANU won all three seats in Tonj, his district. In the 1975 election, I had to be guided by these statistics in deciding how to campaign. I chose one candidate in Gogrial, in addition to myself, two for Tonj and one for Wau. We campaigned together as a team of five and won the five seats. This was a political campaign very close to my heart. There will be many details about this campaign in my other writings, which will follow this book.

To return to the 2010 election contest and the role of General Pieng Deng Majok Kuol Arop in rigging my seat, General Pieng came to Turalei on the eve of polling, in a huge military convoy that befitted an army general going into a military battle, not a political battle. The general gathered the SPLA force that was stationed in Twic before the election, and told the army he had come to Twic to make sure that the SPLA destroyed one particular big black snake there. He did not mention me by name, but there was no mistaking to whom the general was referring, as far as his soldiers were concerned, not just the civilian electorate.

General Pieng then ordered his army to take over the forty-plus polling stations in my constituency: 'No election official should be allowed into any of these polling stations.' The SPLA soldiers were to read out the electoral roll call, name by name, and hand over the voting tokens to other soldiers, which they would then post into the polling box of the SPLM official candidate. In this way, the SPLA soldiers would ensure that only the SPLM candidate was elected, and that this terrible big black snake was defeated.

I had gone to Molbang, the village of my birth, some thirty miles east of Turalei. Returning from my home to Turalei, we criss-crossed with General Pieng on the road. He was heading for Aneet, the temporary headquarters of the local SPLM administration for Abyei.

As I entered my compound in Turalei, I noticed a rather unusual sight. There were a huge number of armed SPLA soldiers there. Their leader quickly approached me and informed me that these soldiers supported me. They had come to talk to me about something to do with the election, which was starting the next morning. For much of the night, I sat down with this rather large contingent, and they told me they were very annoyed with the way General Pieng spoke about me to them, and his plan for the election the next morning: 'We cannot allow you to be defeated in these elections through rigging,' they said.

The SPLA soldiers supporting me had a counter-plan. This was to go out that same night and take over all the polling stations in my constituency, so that the electorate could vote normally the next morning. If the general's SPLA contingent attempted to take over the polling stations in turn, then my supporters would resist, and perhaps fight. This was truly terrifying. What kind of election did the SPLA want to conduct in South Sudan?

Running in my mind was not my winning or losing the seat. Rather, I was thinking of the referendum in the South on self-determination that was to follow this parliamentary election only one year later, in 2011. This was it. Self-determination was what the South Sudanese had been dying for, for nearly fifty years. How could I possibly be part of an action that would spoil this great opportunity for them? I had to do something.

For a long time, my name had been associated with the right of the South to self-determination; since the formation of the Southern Front in 1964. How could that image be tarnished by an action that was associated with me? I did my best to persuade the SPLA soldiers to refrain from doing anything that would prevent the South from exercising self-determination. In the very early hours of polling morning, I succeeded in convincing them. As they were leaving in total disappointment, they were blaming those who had proposed coming to inform me of their plans: 'Did we not tell you that we should not inform this old man about what we wanted to do? Did we not tell you that he would never go along with our idea?'

In spite of the disappointment for my supporters, I had to seriously decide whether or not my name should remain on the list of candidates in an election that was now being so blatantly rigged by the SPLA. I first wanted to see how the polling would actually go in the morning, the first day of the polling. I asked my election agents at all the forty polling stations in the constituency to report to me within the first two hours of the first day of polling, to inform me how it was going. All the reports confirmed that General Pieng's plan was working. The election officials were being asked to leave and the SPLA soldiers were taking over. The electoral roll call was also being taken over by the SPLA, and the voting tokens were being given to the SPLA soldiers to place in the box of their candidate.

Within two hours, I issued an email statement, withdrawing my name from the election. My statement was relayed all around the world, to the disappointment of the governments in both Juba and Khartoum. President Omer Hassan Ahmed el Bashir and First Vice-President Salva Kiir Mayardit were running for the presidency, el Bashir for the Sudan and Salva for the South. Both thought I should not have spoken out about the election in this way; I should have kept quiet about the rigging for the greater good of the country. But I had spoken.

It is always difficult in circumstances like this to know what action is in the best public interest. After the events of December 2013 and the mess that these events have inflicted on South Sudan and its people, who can now say with any justification that it would not have been in the best interest of the people of South Sudan to have postponed the 2010 election in order to allow the country to take more time to prepare better for the new state, than to rush things?

Until General Pieng inflicted on me the blow that has been related here, as one of the sons of the late Chief Deng Majok Kuol Arop, I could have been fooled into thinking that he or his brother Luka Biong Deng Majok Kuol Arop, or even Deng Alor Kuol Arop, for that matter, could do me no harm. Given my personal relations with the late Chief Deng Majok Kuol Arop, his children and his entire family, I had always thought we were one family. I should, of course, have known better. I do now.

I have not had any personal relations with General Pieng Deng Majok Kuol Arop. But in the split moments that chance allowed, as he was pursuing the war of liberation in the SPLA, I have always tried to be supportive of him to my best ability. Perhaps the best example of this was the time I had to demonstrate to him that he had my support as one of the liberation commanders.

In 1998, Commander Pieng almost lost his life in an ambush by the Messiria Baggara Arab militia at a small village in Twic county called Abindau, just a mile or two east of the small town of Wunrok Adiang. It was a horrendous famine time and I was in Wunrok, monitoring food distribution to the local population. While the fighting was raging, Commander Pieng managed to get off his tank, which was being bombarded by the Messiria militia, and escape with his life. The tank and everything else was captured and taken away by the Messiria Baggara Arab militia, known as Muharahlin at that time.

Commander Pieng ran to Wunrok, and without a second thought I offered him all my travelling kit – my tent and all its bedding: a camp bed, mattress, blanket, bed sheets, pillow and two chairs; everything. I had already requested a flight from Nairobi to return to the United Kingdom. I offered him all my sympathy and prayers for his safe escape from the Arab militia, who at that point were a menace to the entire Dinka community across the common borders with Northern Sudan, having been armed, equipped and supplied by Khartoum to cause havoc. I blamed Commander Pieng for the fact that the Arab militia were allowed to take away the SPLA tank, all the way on foot up to Abyei, a journey of many days on foot, without being intercepted by the SPLA. The Messiria militia had towed the tank along with them, pulled by horses, because the tank's engine would not start. They camped, for the first night after capturing the SPLA tank, at a place called Ajoong, less than four miles from Wunrok, where we were all camping. I believed, in my non-military way, that Commander Pieng and his SPLA forces, who had by now regrouped at Wunrok, could have got the tank back from the Messiria if they had staged a night raid on the Arabs at Ajoong.

My close connection and relationship with Commander Salva Kiir Mayardit caused him problems with his leader, Colonel Garang. Our relationship contributed to a final rift between the two leaders of the SPLM, almost resulting in an armed conflict between them. This was only avoided because they agreed to convene a meeting of their movement's leadership in Rumbek, in Bahr el Ghazal, which calmed things down.

Colonel Garang at least once summoned Salva Kiir to a one-to-one session and ordered him to refrain from any connection with me. Salva Kiir told him he could not obey such an order. 'Bona Malwal is one of the leaders and elders of my community. What reason would I give to my people for not relating to Bona?' Colonel Garang told him that I was not a supporter of their movement. Salva Kiir responded by saying that I was a supporter: 'Look at his writings now, in the *Sudan Democratic Gazette* – look at his writings in his previous newspaper, the *Sudan Times*, when he was still living in Khartoum – they all supported the movement.' The confrontation dragged on to the point that Salva Kiir had to give examples of another well-respected South Sudanese leader and elder, Abel Alier Wal Kwai, who was living in Khartoum, the enemy sanctuary. Abel Alier is a close relative of Colonel Garang's wife, and was always invited to their home when he was visiting Nairobi. Indeed, Abel Alier had some influence in persuading Colonel Garang to accept to negotiate peace with the North, to end the long civil war. Despite this example, the conversation remained inconclusive, and Colonel Garang and Salva Kiir Mayardit each continued to see whomever they wanted to see amongst the non-SPLM leaders and elders of South Sudan.

Clearly, Colonel Garang was used to being obeyed by everyone in South Sudan, let alone in his own movement. But the fact that Bahr el Ghazal did not obey the colonel's orders not to have any dealing with me became a frequently recurring thorn in his side as the South Sudan war of liberation dragged on under his command.

In 2004, after the Twic Mayardit community held their first conference at Turalei and elected me as their first community leader, Colonel

Garang could take it no longer, especially as Salva Kiir Mayardit was at Turalei at this time, although he did not attend the conference. So Colonel Garang paid a visit to Twic, his first in his twenty-one years as the leader of the SPLM. Suspecting that Salva Kiir Mayardit had inspired the Twic Mayardit community to elect me, he attempted to discover how the Twic community could have elected me as their community leader in an SPLM-controlled area, when I was alleged to be against the SPLM. In his many meetings with the community leaders, Colonel Garang campaigned for the Twic community to withdraw their support from me.

The leaders of the Twic Mayardit community had their own political agenda for electing me unanimously. They wanted to use their vote for me as a confidence builder, in order to help me to reconcile with Colonel Garang. Sadly, they could not achieve their objective before the colonel met his fate in July 2005. The colonel was not interested in reconciliation – that was not his strong suit. Once he disagreed with you, the only way for him to deal with you was to get rid of you, if that was possible without tracing it back to him.

In January 2005, Colonel Garang had just signed the CPA with Khartoum that ended the twenty-one-year civil war. Under that peace agreement, he had assumed the powerful position of first vice-president of the whole of Sudan, as well as being the first president of the government of South Sudan. Khartoum had no say in whatever Colonel Garang did with certain persons in South Sudan. It was during this very short time – just a mere three weeks in which he was in power over South Sudan – that Colonel Garang showed his hand over his South Sudanese enemies, whether real or perceived. A whole list of SPLA military commanders, headed by no other than Salva Kiir Mayardit, were pensioned off, before even the idea of reorganizing the SPLA as a conventional army for South Sudan came to anyone's mind.

After Colonel Garang's death, in July 2005, the leadership of the SPLM did the only sensible thing it could do at that time – it brought Commander Salva Kiir Mayardit back from retirement and elected him the new leader of the SPLM movement, now the ruling party of South Sudan.

Chapter 6

What I Tried To Do For Abyei

The reason I decided to write this book is to record what I have tried to do for Abyei in my personal and public life. Having been so maligned over the case, by no one other than the Abyei people themselves, I want to offer this chapter as a record of what I did, whenever I could, to help ease their plight. I do this to answer some of the unfounded charges and accusations levelled at me over the years by the young leaders of Abyei. These leaders, some of whom I have mentioned already, have decided that I am responsible for Abyei remaining part of Northern Sudan to this day. By doing so, they are holding an individual responsible for the fate of an entire people without any justification.

Fortunately for me, I have been a political activist in the history of South Sudan, but have never really wielded any absolute power. Since these accusations have been repeated time and again, I have decided to put on record my side of the case. I regard it as my personal duty to have helped the Nok people of Abyei, and in doing what I did I have always been very conscious of my personal and family connection to them.

The leader of my detractors has been Deng Alor Kuol. He has vehemently accused me and insulted me in public and in private for what he says has been my policy of wanting the Ngok people of Abyei not to return to South Sudan from the North after Sudan became independent from Britain on 1 January 1956. I am, of course, personally privy to the CPA policy that defines the border of South Sudan and Northern Sudan, as this was first decided by the Southern Front in 1965: I was the secretary-general of the Southern Front when it was founded in October 1964. It was the Southern Front that called for the right of the South to self-determination, when the first military dictator, General

Ibrahim Abboud, was overthrown in a popular uprising in Khartoum in October 1964. This first-ever progressive movement of South Sudan was founded by a spontaneous mass rally in Khartoum.

At this time the Southern Front insisted that only it should represent South Sudan in that first civilian government of Sudan after the over-throw of the first military dictator. The prime minister of the October 1964 interim government, Sir el Khatim el Khalifa, did not only accept that the Southern Front would represent the South in his government, but he also accepted the appointment of the Southern Front nominees to the positions the Front demanded. Nothing was unusual in any of this. It happened all the time in the politics of South Sudan. The Anya-Nya liberation movement alone represented the South at the 1972 Addis Ababa peace negotiations. Deng Alor Kuol's SPLM alone represented South Sudan at the CPA negotiations of 2005.

The Southern Front appointed Clement Mboro, the most senior South Sudanese administrator, as the minister of the interior in charge of national security. Civil war was raging in South Sudan by then and the Sudanese national army was repeatedly being accused of commit-ting atrocities against the civilian population in the South, in the name of security. The Southern Front had to check this.

The second successful policy of the Southern Front was to commit the interim prime minister, Sir el Khatim el Khalifa, to holding a round table conference before the impending elections in the country to decide on a political solution to the raging civil war in the South. The prime minister accepted both these policies, and the Southern Front began to prepare for these events.

As secretary-general of the Southern Front, I had to be part of its policy-making; hence my problem with those who, for whatever reason, did not accept those policies in full or in part. For instance, to prepare for the Round Table Conference of March 1965, the Southern Front had to decide what type of policy it should present for the future of South Sudan. A national convention in Malakal, the capital of Upper Nile, was held to consider this, and it was decided that the Southern Front should call for the right of South Sudan to self-determination. It was also decided that the political and geographical borders of South Sudan over which the South would exercise self-determination should be the borders of the three provinces of South Sudan with the North as those borders stood when Sudan became independent on 1 January 1956.

This border definition was an important part of the debate at the Malakal convention. This was so particularly because the Abboud military regime had altered some of the provincial borders between the South and the North, after the discovery of minerals in parts of South Sudan. By defining the borders, the Southern Front limited the debate over border demarcation, and at the same time denied the North claiming parts of the South, such as Kafia Kenji, which were part of the South before independence.

It was easy for Colonel Garang and those who negotiated the CPA on behalf of South Sudan at Navaisha, Kenya, in 2005, to simply observe the borders between the South and the North as they stood on 1 January 1956. But for those such as Deng Alor Kuol, who did not like the fact that 1 January 1956 left Abyei in Northern Sudan, this was held as a grudge against me – for the reasons recounted in this book.

For posterity, I need to mention that the 1965 first national convention of the Southern Front at Malakal debated the Abyei situation, and how it related to the struggle of the people of South Sudan against Northern Sudan. There was no divergence between the views and the decision of the convention. Up to that point the debate about Abyei had been purely internal, between the educated citizens of Abyei themselves and without anyone else being involved, either from other parts of South Sudan or from Northern Sudan – the situation being seen in terms of the fact that Abyei was by this time a settled part of Northern Sudan. Most of the political activists of Abyei had been educated in South Sudan schools up to secondary level, whereas most of the children of the ruling family of Deng Majok Kuol Arop had been educated in the Northern Sudan system, including Deng Alor Kuol himself.

Deng Alor Kuol, my main detractor over the Abyei problem, has unfortunately been so successful in his opportunistic political manoeuvrings that one wonders how the Ngok people of Abyei can depend on such an individual to deliver them from their current predicament.

Throughout my life I have aspired to stand with the truth and to do the right thing for my people, including the people of Abyei. I have not tried to win favours by being untruthful. Yet leaders such as Deng

Alor Kuol think more of the opportunities in their hands than the need to stand for the truth.

Deng Alor Kuol, the leader of the Ngok Dinka of Abyei, is believed by his people when he says he will deliver them from their predicament with the North. While his father and mother are authentic Ngok Dinka, Deng Alor Kuol, for all the practical facts of life, is a culturalized Arab Sudanese. His father, Alor Kuol, migrated to Northern Sudan with his family after falling out politically and socially with his stepbrother, the late Chief Deng Majok Kuol Arop.

Clearly, the differences between Chief Deng Majok Kuol Arop and his stepbrother, Alor Kuol, had nothing to do with being assimilated into the Northern Sudanese Arab culture and Islamic religion. Deng Alor grew up in the Gezira area of Northern Sudan, Wad Madani, as culturally an Arab and a Muslim. Fortunately for Deng Alor Kuol, assimilation is something the Arabic culture practises very well. So, without even thinking about it, Deng Alor Kuol adopted Islam as his religion and Ahmed, an Arab name, as his birth name. Known as Ahmed Deng, Deng Alor Kuol grew up in Wad Madani until he completed his secondary education there and won a scholarship to study at a university in Egypt.

Deng Alor Kuol knows nothing about the Dinka and their way of life. But no one in the South really picks on anyone's background – shady or not. So when Deng Alor Kuol's next opportunity beckoned at the start of the SPLM, he joined and somehow found himself as one of the kitchen boys for the leader of the new movement of South Sudan, Colonel John Garang. This is where and how Deng Alor Kuol got his power in South Sudan.

My real problem with Ahmed Deng Alor Kuol was my refusal to be cowed into accepting that South Sudan was fighting to create a 'New Sudan' rather than for its right to self-determination from the North. Even though Colonel Garang had reconciled his political agenda for a 'New Sudan' with the views of his people for self-determination, Deng Alor Kuol continues to believe that the case of the Ngok people of Abyei can be blamed falsely on people such as myself, who continue to say that only by sticking to the facts and the truth of the Abyei case is a political solution possible.

The decision to educate Ngok children in the Northern Sudan system of education was a very deliberate and very important decision taken by Chief Deng Majok Kuol Arop. It demonstrated the seriousness of his Northern Sudan affiliation. The chief decided that his own two sons, Francis Mading Deng Majok Kuol Arop and Zacharia Bol Deng Majok Kuol Arop, who were both doing well in the South Sudanese pattern of education, and had just been accepted to Rumbek Secondary School (the only secondary school in South Sudan at that point), instead had to receive their secondary education in Northern Sudan.

Francis and Zacharia left Rumbek Secondary School and were admitted to Khor Tagad Secondary School in El Obeid, the capital of Kordofan province, to which the Ngok people of Abyei administratively continue to belong, at the time of this writing. This happened when the Ngok people of Abyei were peaceful with their Messiria Baggara Arab neighbours, and the political debate between the South and the North was still at a peaceful level in the parliament at Khartoum, the capital of the country.

Even the remnants of the Torit uprising of August 1955, those who refused to surrender to Khartoum, had suspended their military activities and withdrawn into the hinterland of South Sudan, mainly Equatoria. The revolution of South Sudan had to wait for political decisions to be made. South Sudan was aspiring to self-rule from the North, federation or autonomy; the debate was peaceful and political at this point. In seeking self-rule from Khartoum, the South had accepted, at least temporarily, the colonial decision of 1947, made in Khartoum and later announced in Juba, that the two parts of the country had to be administered as one country. It can also be said that the South had tacitly accepted that South Sudan and Northern Sudan had now become one country. For whatever it was worth, the political leaders of South Sudan at this point had accepted the unity of the country.

It was, therefore, understandable that the ethnic leaders of the Ngok Dinka people of Abyei aspired to improve their relationship with those in Northern Sudan with whom they were now one administration, since the South was no longer going to be a separate state. The unity of South Sudan and the North improved the position of the Ngok people of Abyei when it came to remaining in the North.

Up until the 1965 Round Table Conference in Khartoum, when the Southern Front first introduced the right of the people of South Sudan to self-determination, all political debate in Sudan was about autonomy, all the way to federation. It is, therefore, understandable that the Ngok leaders of Abyei in the SPLM expressed such hate against me. I had been, after all, secretary-general of the Southern Front, the political movement of South Sudan that had for the first time introduced a separatist element into the political debate, a debate that until that time was confined to the South seeking self-rule for itself from the powers-that-be in Khartoum. The introduction of self-determination into the political debate did not only cause problems for me with the Ngok leaders of the SPLM, but it had done so long before with other South Sudanese political leaders, who had viewed the Southern Front as a political movement that was complicating their own party relationship with Northern Sudan.

After the interim government of Sir el Khatim el Khalifa handed over power to the elected government in the North – the elections having been conducted only in the North without the South, because the Southern Front had successfully boycotted them – the Unity Party of Santino Deng Teng went on the rampage in South Sudan, massacring every educated and/or politically enlightened South Sudanese they could find, on the basis that they were all members of the Southern Front and therefore separatists and rebels.

For its part, SANU, under the leadership of William Deng Nhial – which had broken away from the original SANU abroad, the political arm of the Anya-Nya liberation movement, and had returned to Khartoum to pursue a promise of federation by the North – thought that the self-determination policy of the Southern Front was obstructing the attainment of federation for the South from the North. As often in South Sudanese politics, the easy option is to condemn to death your political opponents.

The Sudanese army later captured, and published in the Sudanese media, letters written by William Deng Nhial. These letters called on the Anya-Nya commanders in Bahr el Ghazal to liquidate specific people, me for example, by name! The Anya-Nya movement, which of course was fighting for outright separation from the North, did not take notice of the demands that were being made against the leaders of the Southern Front, because they were calling for self-determination for the South.

Because the SPLM leadership had successfully initiated the policy of liberating the whole of Sudan in order to create a 'New Sudan', the personal antagonism towards me by the Ngok leaders of the SPLM emanated from the fact that I had managed to persuade their leader, Colonel Garang, to include in his ideas the right of the people of South Sudan to self-determination.

As the South Sudanese had not been consulted in any form, the decisions about their political future having always been decided on their behalf by others, and those others always being foreigners, Colonel Garang agreed to include their right for self-determination into the political debate. It was not only the unionist leaders of the Ngok within the SPLM who hated my guts for insisting on this; the Northern Sudanese leaders of the SPLM, from the Nuba Mountains and from the Angesina Hills, all detested me as well.

Until they were finally persuaded to negotiate for peace, because the war had gone on for far too long, the SPLM leadership, from Colonel Garang himself down, had convinced themselves that they were capable of liberating all of Sudan and ruling it. However, the real picture for the hard-core South Sudanese fighting men of the SPLA was different. These young men were fighting to liberate themselves from the North, and their own unionist commanders knew this. So, when I finally managed to persuade Colonel Garang to include self-determination on his agenda, individual members of the Abyei community of the SPLM, such as Luka Biong Deng Majok Kuol, could not contain themselves. Hatred of me broke out, and has remained very strong.

The first occasion when there was an outburst against me was on the day in May 1994 when the SPLM signed an agreement with the leaders of the Umma Party in Chukudum in Eastern Equatoria, an agreement in which the Umma Party agreed for the first time ever to recognize the right of the people of South Sudan to self-determination. Colonel Garang had more than four months earlier authorized me in writing to negotiate in London with the party leaders – Omer Nur el Daim and Mubarak al Fadil al Mahdi.

Colonel Garang had delegated Peter Nyot Kok Malok, who was the representative of the SPLM in Germany, to join me in these negotiations. Since this was the first time an attempt had been made to sell self-determination to a leading Northern Sudanese political party, the feeling within much of the SPLM was that it would not work. No SPLM leader, arguably including Colonel Garang himself, expected that the negotiations would come to anything. If they did not, the failure could have been used against me, since it was I who insisted that these talks be conducted. And if they did not work, then the leadership of the SPLM would have the opportunity to tell me and all those who had aspired for the political right of the South to self-determination to shut up and let the SPLM get on with the war to create the 'New Sudan'.

This idea of 'New Sudan' had become extremely entrenched within the SPLM leadership. Self-determination was seen as a distraction from the cause. And since people like me could not easily be persuaded to give up the idea of self-determination in favour of the 'New Sudan' – and since self-determination for a people who had struggled for it for so long was beginning to gain some attention from the international peace mediators, all of whom wanted peace because war had gone on for so long and the people of South Sudan had suffered from this war for so long – it was better for the SPLM leadership to shut off any mention of self-determination on the grounds that no one in Northern Sudan was prepared to negotiate on it.

So convinced was the leadership of the SPLM about the correctness of their 'New Sudan' policy that they regarded any talk about any other type of policy pursuit as traitorous. A light-hearted example of this occurred after I had finally persuaded Colonel Garang, after three or four months, to call in James Wani Igga, one of the only senior commanders of the SPLA who was present in Kampala, Uganda, where I had been meeting with the colonel. Colonel Garang told Wani Igga that he had decided to authorize me to discuss self-determination with some of the Northern Sudanese political leaders. Wani Igga could not believe what he had heard – that Colonel Garang had authorized me to negotiate with the Umma Party, and that if the results were not satisfactory to the SPLM they would disown these results. Wani Igga told Colonel Garang, by way of a strong warning (since he could not threaten the leader), that if this went wrong it would all fall on Garang's own head. Garang retorted humorously that he had a big head and could carry any weight that might fall on it.

I had the opportunity to recall these events when I visited James Wani Igga at his office in Juba, after he was appointed vice-president of South Sudan. I jokingly asked him, 'How heavy is the position of the vice-president of an independent Republic of South Sudan?' We laughed, and proceeded to discuss other important matters relating to the young state.

Self-determination and my role in pursuing this political agenda had been the core of my political disagreement with Colonel Garang, who as leader of the SPLM had come to dominate the politics of South Sudan. Because he was a strong leader who never brooked a counter opinion, most people of South Sudan had come to respect him, follow him and almost worship him, not because of fear (although there was a bit of that too) but mainly because he had managed the liberation of South Sudan better than anyone else before him.

For individual members of the South Sudanese community like myself, to advance a contrary point of view was seen as detracting from the cause. This was unacceptable, and those who held such views had to be liquidated if possible. This accounts for many of the internal atrocities that were committed within the SPLM.

There is the universal belief that if one's day to die has not arrived one will survive – and this is perhaps what has allowed perceived 'detractors' like myself to have lived on. Efforts to liquidate people were repeatedly planned and attempted. Yet our survival is also down to friends such as, in my case, Salva Kiir Mayardit, who did all they could to protect me.

It is the overwhelming belief in the liberation policies of the SPLM, especially the pursuit of the 'New Sudan' policy, that led to the extreme hate for me by the three young leaders of Deng Majok Kuol Arop's family members of the SPLM – Deng Alor Kuol, Pieng Deng Majok Kuol Arop and Luka Biong Deng Majok Kuol Arop. These three had arrogated to themselves the right to put me down. Their belief in the 'New Sudan' also reinforced their belief in the unity of South Sudan with Northern Sudan, which had been so repeatedly emphasized through the liberation idea. 'New Sudan' also exaggerated the belief in the unity of Sudan amongst most leaders of the SPLM movement from Abyei. This belief in 'New Sudan' may also be the reason why Chief Deng Majok Kuol Arop's children in the leadership of the SPLM continue to sabotage South Sudan.

With the people of the Nuba Mountains and the Angesina Hills now an integral part of the SPLM movement, the liberation of South Sudan, which did not include Abyei and these three areas of Northern Sudan, had to be discouraged, and those who raised the notion of such divisive projects like self-determination, like myself, had to be dealt with – at least vilified verbally, if nothing else.

There was also the internal belief, not expressed openly very often but still present in the Abyei leadership of the SPLM, that since the North would not allow Abyei to revert to South Sudan, then it was in the interest of the leadership of Abyei, wherever they may be, to prevent South Sudan from breaking away from the one Sudan in order to become independent. This point came up very clearly internally and would sometimes be expressed in joking, but extreme, ways.

I recall one such discussion that I had with a few of Deng Majok Kuol Arop's family members at the residence of Francis Mading Deng Majok in Washington DC. I told them that, in my view, we needed to separate the question of Abyei from the political cause of South Sudan. I went on to say that this was because, with Abyei having chosen for such a long time to be part of Northern Sudan, to introduce Abyei into the politics of South Sudan with the North would complicate the liberation of South Sudan.

One of Deng Majok's sons, Arop Deng Majok Kuol Arop, a polite young man from whom I had never heard a rude word, stood up and addressed me in an extremely angry tone. 'You, Bona Malwal, if this is your view about Abyei, then someone should put a bullet through your head.' This was an extremely far cry from what the conversation was supposed to be about. Francis Mading Deng intervened, and rebuked his younger stepbrother for being so rude. The conversation, of course, ended there, and after dinner we dispersed.

Young Arop Deng Majok Kuol Arop came to my hotel the following day and apologized for what he had said the previous evening. After that, he and I resumed our normal relations. I had known this young man very well because he was working with the giant Kenana Sugar Company in Sudan, where we had met quite often.

For myself, I did not find it threatening to discuss the relationship of the political case of Abyei alongside the political cause of South Sudan against Northern Sudan. Threat of physical liquidation for those who do not comply with the policy dictates of the Abyei leaders of the SPLM goes on in South Sudan all the time. Thanks to behaviour like this, it is not so easy to see how much support can be rallied in South Sudan today to resolve the Abyei issue with Khartoum.

My personal stand for the right of South Sudan to self-determination was also the main cause for my disagreement with Luka Biong Deng Majok Kuol. I have never agreed politically with Luka Biong. He has been driven by his belief that he is so powerful in South Sudan that he can put down, with impunity, anyone who disagrees with his own policy line on any topic, and he has always implied that anyone who disagrees with him is doing so at their own risk. Having overplayed his hand in the divided politics of South Sudan, however, he is now a fugitive.

Likewise, my relationship with General Pieng Deng Kuol. After he achieved his electoral objective against me, I never really had any dealings with him. The last time I ever came into contact with him was when he had become the Commissioner General of Police, after he had been removed from the army. He was invited to a celebration organized in my honour by my community, in Juba. General Pieng and I exchanged friendly greetings and chats.

This relationship between me and the children of the late Chief Deng Majok Kuol Arop is not very strong, but I have always had a very close and cordial relationship with much of Deng Majok Kuol Arop's family. This close relationship was not only between me and those of my own generation, Francis Mading Deng Majok Kuol Arop and Zacharia Bol Deng Majok Kuol Arop, but with their late father, Chief Deng Majok Kuol Arop himself. I had always treated any of the children of Chief Deng Kuol Arop, including General Pieng Deng Kuol himself and his stepbrother, Luka Biong Deng Kuol, as my younger brothers, exactly the same way I treated my own brothers and children.

What else did I try to do for Abyei before my present position of not getting involved? Quite a few things, in fact.

Before I was elected to the 1968 national parliament of Sudan, I had already been involved with trying to explain to and persuade Chief Deng Majok Kuol Arop that in the long run South Sudan would achieve a better status in its relationship with Northern Sudan if only by acquiring a degree of a federal arrangement, something that would be tantamount to independence. I had always told him that the Ngok people of Abyei would be better off being part of South Sudan. For me, of course, I had always believed that if such a thing had happened it would cement the traditional connection between our two sections, so rudely separated for many long years by one being in the South, the other in the North. The chief did not, of course, take my advice, but our personal relationship remained good.

When I became a member of parliament for the first time in 1968, an opportunity to serve my uncle Chief Deng Majok Kuol Arop presented itself. Governor Ali Baldo, the most notorious of Northern Sudanese administrators to set foot in South Sudan, had been transferred from Juba – where he had been for a long time a very cruel Governor of Equatoria – to El Obeid as governor of Kordofan, his native province. Ali Baldo was a giant during the Abboud military dictatorship of Sudan, because of the harsh policies he was implementing in South Sudan. The stories about him when he was governor of Equatoria were incredible. Not only did he hate the South Sudanese and punish them at every turn even for crimes they did not commit, but he also made himself into the converter of the South Sudanese to Islam. He began with the chiefs, native chiefs of Equatoria, threatening them that any one of them who did not convert to Islam from no matter what other religion (especially Christianity) would have to lose his position as a chief. Although the native chiefs of Equatoria did not believe in conversion, they gave themselves Islamic names to please him and to protect their jobs. Chief Jambo of the Moru tribe of Mundiri gave himself the Islamic name of Ibrahim, thus becoming Ibrahim Jambo. Chief Jambo was often reported as having asked other native chiefs of Equatoria what their government names were – not their Islamic names. He advised the other chiefs that giving oneself an Islamic name to protect one's job was not a bad thing, if one did not really believe in conversion from one's original belief to Islam.

To get at those educated South Sudanese who actively thought about the political cause of the South, Ali Baldo would find fault with those who were established in their own non-Islamic faith. The classic example of this was Clement Mboro, the most senior South Sudanese administrator, who had been denied by the North the opportunity of benefiting from the Sudanization of civil service posts after the British left. Clement Mboro had become the district commissioner of Juba district of Equatoria. The capital town of Juba district was also Juba town, the provincial seat of Governor Ali Baldo. Clement Mboro did not see eye to eye with Ali Baldo, because he refused to convert from Catholicism to Islam. Then Clement Mboro made the mistake of getting married to a second wife. Ali Baldo seized this opportunity to arrest Clement Mboro, accusing him of marrying a second wife when Christianity forbids it.

To save Clement Mboro from Ali Baldo, he had to be transferred from Juba to Port Sudan, from where he became deputy governor of Darfur, before the Southern Front nominated him as the first South Sudanese minister of interior when the Abboud regime was overthrown October 1964.

In Kordofan, as governor, Ali Baldo missed Southerners to lynch or marginalize. The only one he could find was Chief Deng Majok Kuol Arop, who had by this time become a towering influence in the tribal administration of Kordofan province as a whole, of which his Ngok Dinka people of Abyei had been part since 1905. The chief and his Ngok native administration had for a long time shared a native court with the Messiria Baggara Arabs of Southern Kordofan. The presidency of this court rotated between a Messiria Baggara Arab and a Ngok Dinka chief. It was a happy arrangement for both of the ethnic communities of the area. No one complained, until Ali Baldo arrived as governor.

One of his first decisions was to dismiss Chief Deng Majok Kuol Arop as chief of the Ngok Dinka. Yet the chief was not without some influence in the Sudanese state at that point. Although the Messiria Baggara Arabs of Southern Kordofan had always won the parliamentary seat that they shared with the Ngok Dinka people of Abyei, because their large numbers always outvoted the Dinka, in the 1968 parliamentary elections Chief Deng Majok had complained to the Messiria Chief Babo Nimir that this time around the Arabs should let a Dinka take the parliamentary seat in the interest of friendship, brotherhood and equitable sharing. Chief Babo Nimir, who himself or another member of his family always won this seat, agreed to give the Ngok of Abyei a chance to represent the area in Khartoum. Chief Deng Majok nominated his own son, Ahmed Deng Majok Kuol Arop – his elder son, in fact. With the support of Babo Nimir, Arop won the seat. He became a member of the Umma Party, but of the Al Sadig al Mahdi wing of that party, which was now in opposition in parliament. But Uncle Deng Majok also had me as another of his influences in parliament.

Whatever influence Uncle Deng Majok may have had in Khartoum, Governor Ali Baldo dismissed him from his post as chief of the Ngok Dinka of Abyei anyway. Chief Deng Majok travelled by commercial lorry, with seventeen of his people, from Abyei to Khartoum, in the middle of the rainy season in July or August 1968. Before arriving in Khartoum, he had decided that he would not involve his son, Ahmed. Uncle Deng Majok arrived with his men in front of my small rented home in Khartoum North, as my guests. After taking my wife and young children to the home of a relative so that I could host Uncle Deng Majok Kuol Arop and his men at my home, I went to a cattle ranch in Khartoum and bought a bull and many provisions with which to feed them. Late in the evening, after the people accompanying the chief had retired to rest, I sat down with him to hear what was happening. In his usual distinguished and dignified way, he related to me the humiliation inflicted on him by Governor Ali Baldo.

The chief started with an apology for putting me to such trouble: 'In our Dinka tradition, if one of your age group has a son, one considers that son of one's age group as one's own.' He told me that he and my father were of the same age group; that he was initiated into the grown-up group with my father on the same day. I was therefore his son as I was my father's son.

This was a time of good luck and good fortune for both me and Uncle Deng Majok. I had just won an election to parliament and was

Chief Deng Majok in August 1969, just before he was taken to Cairo, where he died. Standing behind him (from left) are Francis Mading Deng, Bashir Archier (Deng Majok's secretary) and Bona Malwal. (From *The Man Called Deng Majok*, through the courtesy and generosity of the author, Francis Mading Deng Majok Kuol Arop)

secretary-general of a political party that was part of the government of the day, in a very tight balance of power in Khartoum. If Uncle Deng Majok came to ask me to assist him and I had not been able to, it would have been a humiliation for me and an embarrassment for him. But at this point my power base was such that I had not the slightest concern that I might not succeed in helping him.

The Southern Front had been invited into a parliamentary government with ten seats that were always a casting vote in that parliament of 1968–9. Of the ten members of parliament, two of them, Clement Mboro and Hilary Paul Logali, had become ministers of the government. It was I, as secretary-general of the party, who negotiated these positions. The Southern Front had by now become of political age, having been founded since October 1964, with me as its first-ever secretary-general. I had by this time already been re-elected twice to the position.

At the time of deciding whether or not to join the government after the elections of 1968, the unanimous decision of the executive committee of the Southern Front was that the first ministerial post, whatever it was, should go to me. The party would then decide on the second ministerial position. I declined to get into the government at that point, preferring to remain just a member of parliament, in order to accomplish some very urgent matters that my constituents wanted me to undertake. Therefore, I negotiated with the other parties of the 1968 coalition government for two positions – industry and mining for Clement Mboro and labour for Hilary Paul Logali. The two ministers of the Southern Front in the 1968 government had become close personal friends, so I had no doubt that I would succeed in getting Uncle Deng Majok reinstated as chief of the Ngok Dinka of Abyei, whatever accusations Governor Ali Baldo had laid on him.

Having fully absorbed what Uncle Deng Majok's complaint was during that late evening talk with him, I decided then and there how to handle the situation. I told him to go to bed and to rest, and that I would come by in the morning to take him to fix the problem. The following day, I picked him up and drove him to see Hassan Awadalla, minister of the interior. I did not need to involve any of my own Southern Front ministers: I thought it was something I could handle on my own.

Uncle Deng Majok and I were let into the office of the minister of the interior, and I could sense in my uncle a feeling of pride and the restoration of his dignity even before we saw the minister. I introduced them to each other, and after short pleasantries I introduced the subject to the minister. I did not want any investigation into why Ali Baldo had dismissed the chief. I just wanted the governor to eat his words about my uncle, as some vengeance for all he had inflicted on South Sudan when he was Governor of the Equatoria province of South Sudan.

While Chief Deng Majok listened silently, I told minister Hassan Awadalla that this chief was my uncle; that he could not be dismissed by a governor while I was a member of that government. I wanted him reinstated immediately and to be treated as if nothing had happened. The minister could say no more. He saw the seriousness of the situation and the implication of what I had said.

The Southern Front held an important casting vote for the government. If the Southern Front pulled out of the government with its ten votes, the government would fall. The composition of those ten votes was also clear to everyone. The seats had been won after a very fierce leadership competition in Bahr el Ghazal province between the Southern Front and William Deng Nhial's SANU. The political influence of the Southern Front and SANU was also very ethnically based – they were heavily Dinka, hence my personal influence.

At the 1968 election, Bahr el Ghazal, particularly the Dinka districts of that province – Aweil, Gogrial, Tonj and Lakes – was the centre of contestation between the Southern Front and the SANU party inside the country. Confined to the Dinka districts of Bahr el Ghazal, the contest in Bahr el Ghazal became one between William Deng as the leader of SANU and me as the secretary-general of the Southern Front. The result of this election was instructive.

In Tonj, William Deng's native district, SANU won all the three seats, including his own. In Gogrial, my own district, there were also three seats. The Southern Front won all of them, including my own Gogrial North constituency. In the other districts of Bahr el Ghazal, the seats were split between the two parties. In Aweil, the most populous district of Bahr el Ghazal, for instance, with a total of five seats, SANU won three and the Southern Front, my party, won two.

The 1968 election was a total disappointment to the Southern Front in both Equatoria and Upper Nile, where the SANU had no contest with the Southern Front. But because of insecurity, owing to the raging civil war, many of the contests in those two provinces of South Sudan were called off. However, the Southern Front won all the seats that were up for election in those two provinces. Hilary Paul Logali won the crucial seat of Juba town; Henry Bago won his Torit North constituency; and Abel Alier Wal Kwai won his Bor South seat, which included Bor town. Clement Mboro also won his Wau town seat, because of the heavy Dinka vote there for him.

Clement Mboro's Wau seat was another leadership contest between two of South Sudan's most distinguished politicians, Clement Mboro for the Southern Front, against Joseph Ukel Garang, a Luo leader (Jur Chol), who was a prominent member of the Communist Party of Sudan.

The election was the first attempt by the Communist Party of Sudan to win an electoral seat in South Sudan – but they failed.

In the end, the contest in South Sudan was between the two major parties, SANU and the Southern Front: SANU won twelve seats and the Southern Front won ten. SANU decided to join the Umma Party wing of Al Sadig al Mahdi in opposition. The Imam el Hadi al Mahdi wing of the Umma Party had a pre-election agreement to get back into the coalition government with Ismail el Azhari's Democratic Unionist Party if their combined parties could secure a majority. In the event, the two parties failed to gain a majority in the election, hence their invitation to the Southern Front with its ten members to join them in government.

This was the strong position I was in at the time of Uncle Deng Majok's misfortune. When I told the minister of the interior that this chief was my uncle and that for him to be dismissed was not possible, the message was clear. Hassan Awadalla immediately placed a telephone call to Governor Ali Baldo in El Obeid, and without even listening to the reasons that led him to dismiss the chief, the minister simply told Governor Baldo to 'take his hands off Chief Deng Majok'. The minister then told the governor that Chief Deng Majok Kuol Arop had now been reinstated to his position as the chief of the Ngok Dinka of Abyei. The minister also said he was sending the chief back to El Obeid the next day on the police plane. When he landed in El Obeid, he would collect his letter of reinstatement from the governor, and then the plane would return the chief to his home.

It is impossible to describe the atmosphere, and how Chief Deng Majok felt about what was happening to him; regaining his glory in this way. Most importantly, the chief felt that his personal authority over his people could not have been enhanced in a more appropriate manner: leaving his home and community on a commercial lorry in the rainy season, as a dismissed and disgraced person, and then returning back home in glory as a reinstated chief on a plane provided to him by the national authority.

It was sad that when I next met Uncle Deng Majok it was when he returned to Khartoum two years later, in 1970, owing to health reasons. He never recovered from his illness and died just a few weeks later. While he was ill, I visited Uncle Deng Majok at least twice every day, and we always had delightful chats, often about the political relationship between the South and the North. In all these conversations he never uttered a word about the future of his Ngok people of Abyei. Nor did I ever try to engage him in such a conversation. I knew his position on this matter, and although I did not agree with it, I respected it. After all, my personal experiences with the chief, which I have related elsewhere in this work, dated back to 1952. If Uncle Deng Majok still had a total commitment to keeping his Ngok community in Northern Sudan, he had betrayed that a little bit that evening, when he was relating to me his quarrel with Governor Ali Baldo. He said that he now knew who his true people were.

Uncle Deng Majok was later taken by his two sons to Cairo for further medical treatment, but he died there. His body was returned to Sudan and taken to Abyei, where he is entombed.

My personal relationship with Chief Deng Majok dated back a long way. Leaving politics aside, on a personal level, his social uniqueness has more to do with stories about his many wives. Some stories even speak of the number of these wives being in the hundreds. I cannot say whether or not this is true, in spite of the closeness of our personal relationship. The author of the life of Chief Deng Majok is my friend and contemporary Francis Mading Deng Majok, who has written an incomparable life of his father, titled *The Man Called Deng Majok*.

Recalling my personal and social relationship with Chief Deng Majok, I would like to share here the story that he tried to add one of my young cousins, the daughter of my Uncle Manyiel Yuot Atem, to his generous list of wives, having been told of a young beauty in my family. This was how almost all the Dinka chiefs accumulated so many wives. For Chief Deng Majok, once a beautiful girl was mentioned to him that was it: the marriage arrangements were started almost at once.

Since there was no reason to delay the wedding to conduct research into the family background, because the chief knew my family so well personally, the chief gave a hundred cows as a dowry. It was almost impossible for my family to refuse this type of marriage and they had to release the young girl to Chief Deng Majok Kuol Arop immediately as his wife. My young cousin knew clearly what her fate was likely to be if she didn't act quickly. I was in Khartoum by this time, preparing

to travel to the United States on an American Aid programme scholarship to study journalism at Indiana University. My young cousin
– who was now nearly married to the chief, because he had paid the
entire dowry in one go and there was no objection from any member
of my family – eloped with her local lover. They travelled by land to
Khartoum, working out that between South Sudan and Khartoum they
had a month or two travelling as husband and wife, and that I would
not force them to return home to the South for my cousin to be given
away immediately as a wife for the chief. My young female relatives
knew my position through many family conversations with them and
others. I always wanted the girls to get married to men of their own
choice. When they arrived at my home they knew they had made the
right decision. I allowed them to stay in Khartoum, but sent word to my
father and uncles that the girl had arrived at my home with her chosen
husband, and that I would return home to the South with them soon
enough. My message seemed to calm everyone at home, including the
chief. He was known not to give up on these matters of marriage, and
he sent a message to my father. He wanted his new wife, even if she
came back with ten children from the man with whom she had eloped.

I had to rush my vacation to the South to return home with this girl.
After all, I had now come to know that she was pregnant and could only
travel that long distance at a specific period of her pregnancy. I was
also preparing to travel to the United States and needed to take care of
various personal matters.

At home, since Chief Deng Majok had told my parents that he
wanted his wife, no matter when, no one in my family wanted to say
anything to the contrary. Everything depended on my move from
Khartoum.

When I arrived back home with my expectant cousin and her
husband, my father told me I had to visit the chief at his home at Abyei,
preferably with my pregnant cousin, to give her away to Chief Deng
Majok as his wife. But as it happened I was spared the ordeal of a
journey to Abyei. Two days after my arrival at my home in Molbang,
Chief Deng Majok Kuol Arop also arrived there, with a large entourage
of men. He had heard that I had arrived from Khartoum with my pregnant cousin and he wanted his wife. My father and other family elders

did not want to get involved: they wanted Deng Majok Kuol Arop to take his wife. But after three days of very hard discussion with my uncle I persuaded him to have his cattle back with ten of my own, for what the Dinka call *Aweec*. This was to defuse any offence I might have caused, because his cows had been with my family for nearly an entire year. In fact, the chief took back a herd almost double his original hundred, because many of his original cattle had given birth while they had been with us and none of them had died.

Francis Mading Deng does not believe that I could have persuaded his father to give up a wife and yet remain friends afterwards in the way he knew we were. But clearly the chief was a very reasonable man, always cognisant of the truth when it was stated clearly and politely to him, the way I did over the problem of my young cousin. The real problem with any tribal chief in Africa is that he always has the last word, and must be obeyed by the community once the chief has pronounced that last word.

I had a similar experience with my own father over an entirely different matter. While I was a minister during the Nimeiri regime I became political supervisor of the administration of Bahr el Ghazal, my native province. What I did while I held this position was to tour all of Bahr el Ghazal once every three months, to acquaint myself with any administrative problems that needed resolution. It was always a festive affair. I took all the heads of government units in the province with me, so we could deal with the problems on the spot. There were truly lively times on these trips to remember.

On one occasion, I went into a large village in a very religious Muslim community, just twenty-five miles east of Raga Town, the capital of Western Bahr el Ghazal district then. The day before we had driven 250 miles from Wau, the provincial capital, to Raga, the district headquarters. We were proceeding from there to Aweil when I was told of a small Muslim community just off the road on the way to Aweil from Raga. I insisted that we needed to visit this rather isolated community.

At the beginning of the Nimeiri regime a vast programme was undertaken to provide clean drinking water in rural areas. One of the villages that benefited was the one we visited. The local administrators told me there was no road, but I did not believe this. How could the rural water programme reach it if there was not a road? I got behind the wheel of my official Land Rover and drove towards the village. Naturally, everyone else had to follow me. The road was not clearly visible, because it had not been used for some time, but it was still passable. When we arrived, with more than thirty government vehicles, the local community could not believe it. Everyone in the village was frightened, thinking it was an invasion by some enemy forces.

The entire community was sheltering from the hot sun under the trees. The only source of water appeared to be a small pool some six or seven miles away. The women and young men would leave early in the morning to go and spend the day at this single water point, then fill up their water containers and return to the village after sunset. Only then could the women prepare the only meal of the day. No one could wash or bathe at all. The local bore well had been out of service for more than a year, but no one had reported it. The administrators of these people, who were only twenty-five miles away at the district headquarters, did not know that nearly a thousand of their own citizens were suffering from thirst.

I asked the head of the rural water department – a certain Luka Ngor, who was travelling with me – to look into the problem with the bore well. A tiny rubber inside the pump had broken, nothing else. Luka Ngor quickly detected the fault, opened his briefcase and replaced the broken rubber. As he pumped the handle up and down, a flood of water gushed out of the well. The sight was incredible. Everyone rushed to the water point, all at the same time. It was some kind of stampede. Everyone wanted to put their head under the pump to wash their head with all their clothes on. This really was the worst example of utter administrative neglect.

My practice when I was political supervisor of Bahr el Ghazal was to visit my own village as the last stop in these tours. I could then spend a day or two with my father, looking into family matters. As in most places I visited, at my village there was always a public welcome. My father, as the chief of the area, led the reception, which was always followed by public speeches. But he never took part in these, because they were either speeches of praise for what I was doing for the community or complaints about the government, of which I was a

162	ABYEI OF THE NGOK DINKA

representative. My father did not want to be part of any of this. He knew
we would have our family sessions later, where he could raise anything
he wanted in private.

In one of my public responses to the good reception in my village,
I recall that I got carried away by the crowd. I told them that the world
was changing and that even the chiefdom, which was led by my father,
might one day come to pass. Although chiefdom itself is a recent development in terms of the Dinka way of life, the crowd showed surprise
at this. I did not take much notice, but my father did, and he was not
pleased.

When we gathered at my mother's home, the main home so to
speak, because my mother was my father's elder wife and everything
family had to happen there, my father asked me to repeat what I had
said at the public rally early in the afternoon. I could not recall. He
asked me to repeat what I had said about the disappearance of the
system of chiefdom. I told him the remark was merely in passing, but
that as a matter of fact no one can prevent change that comes as part of
human progress; and no one can predict what change will bring in the
future. Then I received my lesson in morality and etiquette. My father
asked me that even if I knew a change was imminent, should it be me
to tell the public? He concluded his lecture by saying that after what I
had said publicly that afternoon, no one in the community was going
to listen to the word of the chief any more. His reprimand concluded
with a slight criticism of the government of which I was a member. He
said that it had a lot to do that it was not doing: 'Before the British colonial administrators left the Sudan at independence, this whole country
of one million square miles was very efficiently run by a handful of
British district commissioners. Look at how many ministers you have
in your government, and the country is not running well at all.'

Like most tribal chiefs in Sudan, my father was very critical of
the fact that Nimeiri had dissolved native administration in Northern
Sudan. He lived very much in the great nostalgic era of the colonial native administration of Sudan, South and North, when he and
Northern Sudanese native administrators such as Chief Babo Nimir of
the Messiria Baggara Arabs could resolve any small or large disputes
that arose between their native communities.

Addis Ababa Agreement

My next encounter with the political and social problems of the Ngok people of Abyei came during the implementation of the 1972 Addis Ababa Peace Agreement between the government in Khartoum and the Anya-Nya liberation movement of South Sudan. After Colonel Nimeiri seized power in the military coup of 1969, he dissolved parliament and all the political parties and disbanded the press, including my own newspaper, *The Vigilant*. I sought to leave the country. Influenced by Joseph Ukel Garang, the leading South Sudanese lawyer who had become the most influential member of the Sudan Communist Party, I was banned from departing, and my passport was withdrawn. When I asked the first minister of the interior, Colonel Faroug Amin Alla, he told me that the ban was issued by President Nimeiri himself, on the request of Joseph Ukel Garang. I left the matter there. I had no intention of engaging in any conversation or contact with this military regime, which had dissolved the parliament to which I was elected for the first time; it had dissolved my political party of which I had been a principal founding member; and it had disbanded my newspaper.

But this new, seemingly ruthless regime had also chosen one of my closest political associates, Abel Alier Wal Kwai. Abel became Nimeiri's first minister for supplies in his first government. It became clear, to me at least, that Nimeiri chose Abel Alier as a way of accommodating the political point of view of the South, rather than bringing the political influence of the South to bear on the new system. That Southern Sudan influence was preserved for Garang. Nimeiri charged him with the responsibility to bring forward, within two weeks, the regime's first policy on the South.

I had been in Bahr el Ghazal when Nimeiri seized power, and returned to Wau three days later. Nimeiri had decreed that any member of parliament who was not in Khartoum at the time of his successful military coup should not return there, and Wau, the capital of Bahr el Ghazal, was the furthest I could get from my constituency.

I was quite happy that Nimeiri had appointed Abel Alier, a close personal friend and political associate, but I was not terribly pleased with the fact that Nimeiri had given Southern affairs to Garang, a communist, and not to Abel Alier. These appointments were clearly driven by political accommodation and influence. For accommodation, Nimeiri chose Abel Alier. But for influence, it was disturbing that he was promoting the communist influence in the South.

Abel Alier went into hiding in Khartoum as soon as he learned of his appointment into the cabinet of the new regime. I immediately surmised that he would have wanted to know my personal view, amongst those of others, as to whether or not I thought he should take up this new position. But how to communicate with me was his problem. Since he had not yet decided to take the job, and was therefore not yet a member of the new government, he could not ask that government to allow me to return to Khartoum. Time was ticking away and I had to do something, so I wrote a four-page letter to Abel Alier, advising him to take the job immediately. 'This is still a very dark political picture,' I said. 'In such circumstances, an individual could save the day. If that turns out to be the case, then there is no better individual than Abel Alier to save the day for South Sudan. If not, then South Sudan had no better than Abel Alier to sacrifice.' When he received my letter Abel Alier immediately came out of hiding, went to the palace and took the oath of office as minister for supply in the new regime's first cabinet.

The first task Abel Alier performed as a member of the new government was to send instructions to Wau for me to be allowed to travel back to Khartoum. Political opinion there was in turmoil. The man calling the shots, as far as the politics of South Sudan were concerned, was Joseph Ukel Garang. Whether or not he was sharing his ideas about the new Southern Sudan policy was not material to me. But it was clear to every enlightened South Sudanese that the new South Sudan policy of the new regime would be communist-influenced. Garang put together his team of advisers and included me in the team. I declined. He took offence at this, and ordered that I should not be allowed to leave the country.

Garang sounded out South Sudanese public opinion about his new regime policy for the South. He convened several meetings, most of which I attended. Garang's view was that the South should publicly support regime change in the country. The view that finally prevailed in these meetings was that the regime should first publicly state its policy on the South, especially as it related to dealing with the civil war that was already raging there.

In the end, on 9 June 1969, Nimeiri announced his South Sudan policy: that the regime would pursue peaceful resolution of the conflict in the South. But pursuit of peace was heavily laden with communist jargon, such as that the Sudanese state would pursue the establishment of a regional and international socialist way for the economic development of the country. As Garang embarked on the implementation of his socialist ideals in South Sudan, it soon came to pass that the Communist Party of Sudan had come to lock horns ideologically with other policy trends that were also participating in the Nimeiri regime. These included the pan-Arabist, or Arab socialist supporters of Jamal Abdel Nasser's Arab socialism. Indeed, Nimeiri himself, as a free army officer, was a publicly professed Nasserite. Each of these groups wanted to elbow the others out of the regime, but the members of the Communist Party thought they had the upper hand.

By this time, Nimeiri had begun to turn to the Soviet Union as his principal ally. The communists took advantage of this, and because he had not fully embraced communist ideology as the main policy tenet of his regime, they sought to overthrow Nimeiri by an internal military coup. This took place over three days in November 1971, Nimeiri being detained in the presidential palace. As always happens in circumstances like this, the communists revealed their hand very strongly when they announced their coup leadership. This consisted of three communist members of Nimeiri's former ruling military council: Colonel Babiker el Nur as head, and Colonel Hashim el Atta and Colonel Faroug Amin Alla – all of them well-known communist officers of the Sudanese Army.

Unfortunately for the communists, all three top brass were out of the country. They were in London and due to fly back to Khartoum on a British Airways flight. At this time, British Airways flew to Khartoum from Europe through Libyan airspace. Muammar Gaddafi was still a close personal friend to Nimeiri. Both Gaddafi and Nimeiri had been plotting an Arab states union between their two countries and Egypt, with Gamal Abdel Nasser of Egypt as the head of a United Arab States. Nasser had learnt from his earlier rushed union with Syria. He stalled.

Gaddafi ordered his military jets to force down the British Airways flight in which the leaders of the Sudanese coup were travelling. He arrested the Sudanese Communist leaders of the coup and handed them over to Nimeiri in Khartoum.

When the news reached Khartoum that Gaddafi had intervened on behalf of Nimeiri, officers and men of the tank command of the Sudanese army stormed the presidential palace and freed Nimeiri. All hell broke loose. In anger and vengeance, Nimeiri executed the three leaders of the coup, as well as at least two civilian leaders of the Communist Party of Sudan, Secretary-General Abdel Khalig Mahgoub and Minister of Southern Affairs Joseph Ukel Garang, who had been a minister with Nimeiri since May 1969.

After this dramatic upheaval, Nimeiri appointed Abel Alier as his minister for Southern Sudan affairs and ordered him to start the peace process with the South immediately. Within three months, the March 1972 Addis Ababa Peace Agreement was signed with the South. Abel Alier led the official delegation on behalf of the Nimeiri regime.

While the problem of the Ngok Dinka of Abyei had not been a specific item on the Addis Ababa agenda, because the negotiators, particularly Abel Alier himself, were sensitive to the fact that Abyei had been for a long time part of Northern Sudan and not part of the South. Nevertheless the Addis Ababa peace document mentioned that with the full consent of the central government of Sudan the Ngok people of Abyei would be consulted again, to ascertain that they still wanted to remain part of Northern Sudan rather than reverting to the South, which they had left of their own free will in 1905.

Although I did not play any part in the actual negotiation of the Addis Ababa Peace Agreement, Abel Alier wrote to me while I was completing my master's degree in journalism and international affairs at Columbia University in New York, asking me to go to London in November 1971 to meet the leaders of the Anya-Nya movement in exile, Enoch Mading de Garang and Lawrence Wol Wol. Alier asked me to persuade these two Anya-Nya leaders to take peace negotiations with the Nimeiri government more seriously. I wrote back to Abel Alier in Khartoum, accepting the assignment, and asked him to include Francis Mading Deng on the trip with me. Francis and I went to London, and spent much of November 1971 talking to the Anya-Nya leaders.

By the time the Addis Ababa Peace Agreement was agreed upon and the Anya-Nya leadership had returned to the country, Abel Alier asked me to return home to take part in the implementation of that agreement. I declined to return immediately, because I had only a few months left to complete my degree.

When I finally returned home in July 1972, the implementation of the peace agreement was almost five months old. Abel Alier had been appointed first president of the High Executive Council for South Sudan in Juba, while also remaining vice-president of the Republic of Sudan. He had been promoted to the position after returning from Addis Ababa, having successfully negotiated the peace agreement with the South. A rather nice reward for a one-month job!

I was offered a choice of several posts by Abel Alier when I finally returned home from the United States in July 1972. But I prepared to stay in Khartoum to acquaint myself with the working of a military dictatorship, whose leadership I had not known. This was instead of going to the South as most Southerners were preparing to do, which soon turned into infighting for the political leadership of the South.

I became minister of information and culture in Khartoum and so had no way of not confronting the problems of the Ngok people of Abyei. Political and social problems had by now begun to mount. By 1965, small wars between the people of Abyei and the Messiria Baggara Arabs were becoming frequent.

By this time Francis Mading Deng Majok Kuol had been appointed by Nimeiri as Sudan ambassador to Scandinavia, based in Stockholm, Sweden. He frequently travelled back home to Khartoum and we coordinated the type of action we had agreed to take over the Abyei problems.

My real problem was how to persuade Nimeiri to see the plight of the Ngok people of Abyei and to respond to it. For more than two years, Nimeiri refused to get involved, calling it a local administrative matter for the people of Kordofan. It was difficult to overcome the intransigence of some people, such as Jafaar Mohamed Ali Bakheit, himself a native of Kordofan and minister of local government, under whom fell the local administration of native communities, and Mohmoud Hasseb, the commissioner of Kordofan, from the Nuba Mountains and a close personal friend of President Nimeiri from their military days. I had to play a very patient long game.

When Nimeiri finally agreed to do something about Abyei, he told me that he would personally visit the region and announce his policy there. Nothing could have been more pleasant for me to hear.

Francis Mading Deng and I carefully coordinated the kind of steps President Nimeiri would announce while visiting Abyei. We agreed that Abyei should be removed from the administration of Kordofan and administered directly under the presidency of the republic from Khartoum. We also agreed on the local administrator from Abyei, Justin Deng Aguer, whose ability and character we both knew. It was now a question of planning Nimeiri's visit to Abyei. It was not something we could entrust to the local administration in Kordofan, as we knew their attitude. We had to involve local input from the people of Abyei themselves.

I assigned three Land Rovers from the Ministry of Information to take the Ngok students of the University of Khartoum and others to their own community in Abyei to prepare for the visit of President Nimeiri. The complaints about this visit, from El Obeid, the capital of Kordofan and from Khartoum, even from Nimeiri's own presidential palace, were many, but nothing that we could not overcome.

Even Juba, the regional administration of South Sudan, which I thought I was offering a helping hand to, in resolving a problem that had been nagging them, were not happy with what they thought was a personal intrusion by me into their own affairs. Abel Alier himself, whom I thought would be happy with steps to resolve the Abyei problem and whom I was personally keeping in the picture, was apparently not happy. He ruled himself out of President Nimeiri's visit to Abyei, even though he was always ready to receive President Nimeiri in any part of South Sudan.

The plan in the presidential palace in Khartoum was that the president would fly in his jet to Wau, and then he and his entourage would get into three helicopters to fly to Abyei, a half-hour flight. As had become traditional on such visits by the president to the South, Abel Alier was expected to be in Wau to receive him, even if he did not want to accompany Nimeiri to Abyei. But when we landed at Wau he was

Initiates during their recovery period, their heads covered with palm hats, a
bundle of sorghum stalks in the place of spears, with a musical instrument
made of gourd. (From *The Man Called Deng Majok*, through the courtesy
and generosity of the author, Francis Mading Deng Majok Kuol Arop)

not there, although it did not seem to matter and neither did it seem to
bother President Nimeiri.

When we landed at Abyei the local reception was impressive. Even
those saboteurs of the Abyei plan who had travelled to Abyei with us
from Khartoum and El Obeid were very pleased. The entire Ngok
Dinka community had turned out. The newly initiated young men of
the Ngok community, with their new head markings, were present in
full force.

Never did it occur to me, no matter what the student politics were at
the University of Khartoum, that the Ngok students of Abyei studying
there would work to sabotage a plan that was in the interests of their
own people. But they had taken over the welcoming statement from the
local community of Abyei and wrote it their way, abusing the president

of the republic. The entire gathering was shocked. The students' statement was as highly emotive as it was abusive. The president was asked
what had brought him to Abyei, a foreign Dinka country, which had
no resemblance to an Arab land. 'Did you not see the difference when
you landed? This Dinka country is all wood, river and pasture. This is
not an Arab land; this is a Dinka land!' The statement went on and on.
Nimeiri was sitting motionless, breathing fire.

When the president came to speak, he made the shortest speech
I ever heard him give in the eleven years I was with him in government. He directly addressed me: 'Bona Malwal, so you have brought
me here for your people to insult me and the entire Arab world! I am
not going to do anything for these people of Abyei. Abyei stays part
of Kordofan. I am returning back to Khartoum with everything that
I had brought for these people.' And that was the end of the speech.
Nimeiri climbed down from the speaking platform, climbed into the
military scout car and ordered everyone who had come with him from
Khartoum to leave.

The Ngok community had prepared the most scrumptious meal
of their entire life as lunch for the president of the republic and his
entourage, many of whom had never been to Abyei before. The gloating
ministers from Northern Sudan who had come with us all the way from
Khartoum noticed that I was not in the car. Embarrassed and ashamed
of what my people had done, all I could do was to go and sit alone under
a shady tree. When Nimeiri saw me sitting there alone he shouted to me
to get in the car so that we could leave. I stood up, walked towards him
and told him as politely as I could that I was not going with them – and
that the way he had reacted to this very shameful behaviour from the
Ngok students was not the way I thought he should react as the president of the country.

I told him that the Ngok community had welcomed him into their
midst in the best Dinka tradition possible, as the reception proved, and
that they had had no hand in the plot to spoil his visit. It was entirely
organized by outsiders! I told him that it was not right to take away the
Ngok people's guests without allowing these guests to take the lunch
prepared by the people of Abyei on their behalf. Nimeiri got out of his
car and told the ministers to have their lunch. But he said he was not

going to have lunch with the people of Abyei, because he had been insulted. He went and sat alone under a tree.

This was my opportunity to urge the Ngok chiefs and elders to go and apologize to Nimeiri and to talk to him. I told them that this was the end of the road for them if they did not do so. The Ngok chiefs and elders acted magnificently. They all crowded around Nimeiri under the tree, and Chief Deng Macuei Kuol Arop, the most senior and the most elderly, began to talk. He apologized very profusely, and told Nimeiri that they had no hand as chiefs and elders in what their educated children had done. After all, he said, as chiefs and elders of Abyei they did not know how to read or write, and could not have been part of the rude statement that their educated children from Khartoum had written.

Chief Deng Abot then addressed the refusal of Nimeiri to eat lunch with them. He said that by refusing to have lunch with them, the president had cursed the entire Ngok community: 'You are our head of state. A head of state is a spearman, the spiritual leader of the country. When a head of state or a spiritual leader refuses in anger to eat with his people, he has cursed that people. This is exactly what you, Mr President, have done to the Ngok people of Abyei.'

The chief did not even ask Nimeiri to change his mind and to have lunch with the Ngok community. Nimeiri was so moved and so impressed by what the chief said that he ordered the people to bring him lunch. He then invited me to join him.

While we were having lunch, Nimeiri laughed at me for having been hoodwinked by the Ngok students. The situation had so nicely returned to normal that it was quite possible I could have persuaded Nimeiri to change his mind about the decisions he had already made in Khartoum about Abyei, which he had been prepared to announce in his public statement had he not been prevented from doing so by the students' behaviour. But I was also so personally annoyed that I was not prepared to persuade him to announce his decisions.

We returned to Khartoum that same afternoon and, as far as I was concerned, that was the end of my personal involvement with the Abyei issue, although Francis Mading Deng Majok Kuol and I continued to talk and think about Abyei whenever Francis brought up the topic and wanted my opinion on the matter. Then came the attitude of Deng

Majok Kuol Arop's children in the leadership of the SPLM, and the repeated accusations against me, as related in much of this book.

In spite of all the abuse and insults that continue to be heaped on me, even after I have declared publicly that I have stepped aside from South Sudanese politics to do other things such as writing, I am still very concerned about the plight of the Ngok Dinka people of Abyei. I continue to pray for a workable solution to their predicament. The fact that Khartoum and Juba have ceased to communicate effectively makes the quest for that solution difficult, but it is the only way out and a solution must be found. The fact that Deng Majok Kuol Arop's children, leaders of the SPLM, have misbehaved so much with everyone whose help they need in resolving this situation cannot serve as an excuse not to find a lasting and peaceful solution for the Ngok people.

The arrogance and the uncouth behaviour of the SPLM leaders from Abyei has created an ambivalent attitude about the role of South Sudan as related to the Ngok people of Abyei. How the people of the South feel about the resolution of the Abyei problem is not a question that is easy to answer. Clearly, the people of South Sudan have no problem with the Ngok Dinka people of Abyei in general, which is why the people of South Sudan have tolerated the domination that Deng Majok Kuol Arop's children are practising in the leadership of the South Sudanese government, even before their own land of Abyei has become part of South Sudan.

In more recent times in South Sudan, both Deng Alor Kuol and Luka Biong Deng Majok Kuol have clearly become part of the opposition group that attempted, in cooperation with Riek Machar Teny, to storm by force of arms the seat of the young elected government of South Sudan and to install themselves back in power over South Sudan. When Riek Machar Teny's coup failed in Juba and Deng Alor Kuol and his rebel SPLM group were arrested, their friends around the region and beyond pleaded with the president of South Sudan to free them for compassionate reasons, which he did. They are now part of the transitional government of national unity as part of the newly imposed peace agreement in South Sudan. It is not easy to say that this imposed peace agreement can be maintained in the South.

Elsewhere in Africa, when a group has failed to make a successful coup against a legitimate government of a member state of the OAU, before even attempting to take any steps towards restoring peace to that country the OAU usually condemns the coup attempt. Efforts to restore peace to the country can then follow! Nothing like that happened in South Sudan after the events of 15 December 2013. IGAD simply decided that it wanted to restore peace to South Sudan amongst equals – the legitimately constituted government of South Sudan and the rebellion against the legitimate government. By that type of behaviour IGAD, as a regional organization, has not only added to the illegitimacy that is challenging South Sudan, but more seriously has encouraged the next would-be rebel in South Sudan.

Chapter 7

The Way Forward in Abyei: Back to Basics

It is not right to throw the future of any people into question, no matter how few they may be. I am not going to do that to the Ngok people of Abyei here. Any people have a future, no matter how bleak it may appear to those in charge of that future. Clearly, the previous chapters of this book have indicated that the earlier leaders of Abyei thought of what was best for their people, much more than the current leaders, who misuse the power that they think they have. The misfortune for the Ngok Dinka people of Abyei is that their fate is in the hands of people who now use the situation to exercise power against perceived opponents, rather than exercising it to create friends amongst those who can help to resolve and normalize matters.

The situation of the Ngok Dinka people of Abyei has deteriorated to the extent that it is foolhardy for anyone to think that they have an easy solution. But all concerned must continue to think of possible ways out of this human tragedy.

It is impossible to imagine that external intervention, even if it were feasible, could be a way out. The UN force currently stationed in Abyei has been unable to secure the area so that ordinary citizens can begin to build their lives as free and secure residents of their own land. The insecurity is so extreme that their late senior chief, Kuol Adol Deng Majok Kuol Arop, was ambushed and assassinated by Messiria Baggara Arab militia men as he left the Arab camp, where he had gone in search of peace. This is just one example of the insecurity that Abyei has come to expect.

The chief was brought up in the same, very distinctive, mould as his father, Chief Deng Majok Kuol Arop. Educated in the Northern Sudanese system of learning and culture, he was always as at home with his Messiria Arab counterparts as he was with his Dinka brethren, south of the border. If the Messiria Baggara Arabs truly wanted peace, then the one individual to keep alive was the chief. After his loss, someone else is urgently needed as a go-between.

So difficult is the situation in Abyei now that the only way by which the joint United Nations and Africa Union force currently in charge of maintaining security in Abyei can keep the peace is to create a buffer zone between the two sides. Unfortunately, this buffer is within the geographical territory of the Ngok Dinka of Abyei. Each of the two sides claim it as theirs, and this has yet to be resolved. The Ngok Dinka territory is so small – and the border with its neighbour is so long – one of the longest in the world – that the only route to peace and security is one that allows the Ngok Dinka of Abyei to settle and enjoy their land in peace, through an agreement that both sides are fully committed to.

The Abyei situation may very well be a political problem now in that it involves two independent countries that will not communicate with each other on the matter. On their part, the Ngok leaders of the people of Abyei, who see themselves as rulers of South Sudan, seem to believe that the only way to get rid of the problem is to defeat not only the Messiria Baggara Arabs but also the government in Khartoum by military force. Clearly, the two states – the new state of South Sudan and Northern Sudan – seem happy to allow what is clearly an ethnic conflict between the Messiria Baggara Arabs and the Ngok Dinka of Abyei to continue to rage.

Credible states do not allow ethnic conflicts to ruin relations between them. They sort out these conflicts and hold those on their own side responsible for abiding by the rules of the game that are jointly agreed upon. Neither Khartoum nor Juba is doing this. Each of them is looking for an excuse to hold the other responsible for the failure to resolve the conflict. Because neither party is taking responsibility for resolving the Abyei issue, the situation can and will get out of control unless there is external intervention that will make the two sides see sense.

The Ngok leadership of the SPLM has attempted to internation-alize the case of Abyei, not only by taking it to the International Court of Arbitration in The Hague, but also by making claims for territory that never belonged to the Ngok. The international rulings that have followed have only complicated the issue, and at the time of writing the borders between the two countries have yet to be agreed upon.

Nearly ten years after the signing of the Abyei protocol, it is clear that if the leaders of the people of Abyei and the leaders of the Messiria Baggara Arabs care about the long-term future of their people and the peace and stability of this territory, they need to go back to basics. Each side has invested too much time, energy and resources in trying to overcome the other. Experience elsewhere has shown that problems like this cannot be solved by one side overcoming the other, by force or any other means. A credible and lasting solution is always a mutually agreed one, to which each side commits itself on a permanent basis. Only then can peace and lasting mutual tranquillity be achieved. And surely there are enough points of reference to return to if we are seeking a peaceful resolution to this problem.

The Messiria Baggara Arabs make a big show about their having invited the Ngok Dinka of Abyei to settle on their land. Such utterances are an exaggeration. The same can be said about the claims of those leaders of Ngok who lay claim to some deserted part of the Baggara land.

While it is true that, at the end of each rainy season, not only the Ngok Dinka of Abyei but even the Twic and other Dinka communities beyond Ngok temporarily migrate with their livestock towards the border areas between the Ngok Dinka and the Messiria Baggara Arabs, these movements were always so well regulated and well adhered to that no community made a claim on the land of another simply because they had been allowed to temporarily migrate to escape a bad season. Migratory movements of tribes with livestock, which follow pasture and water, cannot be converted into claims to ownership or possession of land.

Historians and scholars know when the Arabs as a people came to Sudan and who they found there. No one is questioning the right of the Arabs to whatever land they occupy in the Sudan today, but it cannot be said that this was Arab land before the Dinka arrived. It is well documented that the Arabs found the Nilotic tribes of South Sudan – the Dinka, the Nuer and the Shilluk, in particular – there on the land. The migrating Arabs from the Arabian Peninsula conquered and pushed back the Nilotics, to the settlement points that these Nilotic communities now occupy. The Arabs did not come from the South and there had not been land that they had ever occupied southwards, which they had allowed the Ngok Dinka community of Abyei to occupy out of kindness and generosity.

In order to settle the current land dispute, the first thing to do is to settle the political issue. No one in either Northern Sudan or South Sudan can deny that at least the educated and enlightened leaders of the Ngok Dinka community of Abyei have been aspiring for a long time to return to South Sudan, where their kith and kin are. Because their former leaders decided in 1905 to be part of Northern Sudan, it is now essential to have a referendum in Abyei, to decide in a free and fair vote, whether or not they still want to remain in Northern Sudan or to return to South Sudan. Once the Ngok people of Abyei have voted to return to South Sudan (if they do so), then, by political and peaceful agreement, the leaders of both countries should sit down and redraw the borders. Fortunately, this way forward is laid out in the 2005 CPA.

Colonel John Garang, who negotiated the CPA to bring independence to South Sudan in July 2011, did well for everyone because of how he negotiated the Abyei peace protocol. He could not have got away with the claim that the Ngok people of Abyei should return to South Sudan, but at the same time he could not have denied the people of South Sudan the right to self-determination until the Abyei issue had been resolved through a referendum. Finally, there was no way anyone could talk of self-determination in the way South Sudan had been talking about it since March 1965 (at the Round Table Conference) without indicating under what type of borders one should exercise self-determination. This is why the Southern Front had to decide, at its Malakal national convention in February 1965, just one month before moving to Khartoum to table self-determination at the Round Table Conference, that the borders between Northern Sudan and South Sudan should be those that had been set and administered for more than sixty years by the British. If the Southern Front in 1965 and Colonel Garang after them had not insisted on the colonial borders, self-determination may not have taken place and the current disputes, such as the Abyei dispute, would have remained superfluous.

The very clear decision of the CPA to consult the people of Abyei about where they wanted to be is the only workable solution to the Abyei problem. Other suggestions, including the use of force to return Abyei to the South, cannot work.

If Colonel Garang had not died in that helicopter crash, only three weeks after the implementation of the CPA that he had diligently negotiated, the way forward would not have been as murky as it has been made since. One can only hope that the Ngok leaders of Abyei eventually see the logic of this position.

After wasting nearly ten years, and with the loss of so many innocent lives, the country needs to go back to basics. The only thing that is not possible – which the political leadership in South Sudan, with prompting by Deng Majok Kuol Arop's offspring leaders of the SPLM tried to do – is to get away from the basics of the Abyei protocol.

The world needs to tell the leaders in Juba and Khartoum that the Abyei protocol was not intended to be a weapon of war. The protocol was intended to ascertain the wishes of the Ngok Dinka people of Abyei. Do they want to remain in Northern Sudan, or do they want to return to South Sudan? This is such a straightforward document that even the peacekeeping force which roams South Sudan today, without much effect, could easily conduct the referendum.

So why does the international community, which is a signed witness to the Abyei protocol, drag its feet? Only after the Ngok Dinka people of Abyei have voted to return to South Sudan may the international community need to undertake another step, that of demarcating the borders. This is something the international community needs to resolve anyway, since the two states do not seem willing to cooperate to do it themselves, and it is likely that the matter will disturb regional peace, if not world peace. But let us first have the Abyei plebiscite.

The resolution of the Abyei conflict requires some regional intervention, since the two Sudanese parties are not prepared to resolve matters without rancour. Clearly, the solution must be based on the Abyei protocol. Both governments are bound by this. Both need to implement it in full. Any sections that remain outstanding must be implemented.

IGAD, which successfully spearheaded and mediated the CPA, also has an interest in what is currently going on in South Sudan. IGAD should maintain that interest until the CPA is implemented in full. The international community, represented by the troika countries – the USA, UK and Norway, which have acted almost as guarantors, or at least monitors, of the way in which the two Sudans were implementing the CPA – is also required to ensure that the CPA is implemented. Unfortunately, these countries do not seem to have played a constructive role, so far. Naturally, they have their own interests in the two countries and may, from time to time, take sides instead of being impartial.

If the Ngok people decide they want to return to South Sudan, then IGAD should set up a boundary demarcation commission. It should be clear to IGAD, the troika and the international community at large that neither Khartoum nor Juba are willing and ready to find a solution without external involvement.

For the AU, IGAD and the international community to help resolve the Abyei issue, and any other issues of the CPA that remain outstanding, there are certain conditions that need to be adhered to. Both Khartoum and Juba need to be asked to refrain from allowing any of the citizens in the area of conflict to wield power for either of the two neighbouring countries.

In South Sudan in particular, it has not been possible for the government to discuss terms for resolving the Abyei problem without these terms being dictated by the Ngok leaders of the SPLM. Khartoum has interpreted this as Juba giving up its power in this area to the Ngok leaders.

On its part, Khartoum has tried to recruit the Messiria Baggara Arab leaders to be spokesmen for the resolution of the Abyei issue, even though Khartoum has not given the Arabs the type of power Juba has bestowed on the Ngok leaders of the SPLM.

The Abyei leaders of the SPLM have played the military weapon against the North in a way that has made the Messiria Baggara Arabs vie for war with them. Yet the leadership in Juba continues to acquiesce in the misuse of its authority by Deng Majok Kuol Arop's children within the SPLM.

It has always been puzzling to me why the SPLM leaders from Abyei cannot see that the only solution to the Abyei problem is a peaceful one. Anyone who knows the Messiria Baggara Arabs and their characteristics ought not to play with war as a game, in the way the leaders of the Ngok people of Abyei within the SPLM have done. Ten years have been wasted because the Ngok leaders have had a one-track mind – aiming to return Abyei to the South through war. They have tried three times and they have failed. Yet they will not give up. And no one wants to tell them to do so.

If the Ngok people of Abyei think war will succeed, they have not considered the numbers. You can be as brave as you can imagine, but if you do not have the numbers you will never succeed.

One of the problems on both sides is an overstatement of rights. This is shared by most leaders of the SPLM. To create the impression that the Abyei situation is a dispute between the governments and people of Northern Sudan and South Sudan is a mistake that must be retracted in order to find a constructive solution.

Since 1905, Abyei has been part of Northern Sudan by the choice and design of the people of Abyei. They reaffirmed this at the 1952 conference, witnessed by the departing British colonial administrators. It was on this concrete basis that the Southern Front demanded the right of the people of South Sudan to self-determination in 1965. The situation may only have changed now because since 1965 the Messiria Baggara Arabs have not treated the Ngok people of Abyei as equals, let alone as brothers and sisters. It was because of this that Colonel Garang, acting as leader of South Sudan, successfully included in the CPA a special protocol for the resolution of the Abyei predicament.

The Abyei protocol cannot be carried out without the cooperation of the two governments involved. For this to work, the government in Juba must refrain from placing its power and authority in the hands of the Ngok leaders of the SPLM. At the same time, if there are Messiria Baggara Arabs holding power in Khartoum, then Khartoum should remove them from power and not hand them the responsibility of negotiating the implementation of the Abyei protocol. Only by coming clean on who holds power in both Juba and Khartoum can we expect a respectable and implementable solution.

On their part, the international community should continue to be part of the search for how to implement the protocol. This is something the international community should be able to complete with ease, if the two governments cooperate and the international community is serious about seeing the project through. Having helped the CPA to be a document that regulates relations between Khartoum and Juba, the international bodies should not stand by and watch the situation in Abyei fall apart.

Unfortunately, some serious mistakes have been committed that Khartoum has taken advantage of. It was clear from the onset that even before South Sudan seceded Khartoum was being treated as a rogue regime whose sovereign political system needed to be changed without due process. Unfortunately, all the leaders of the Ngok community inside the SPLM saw themselves as the agents for this change of regime that has clearly failed. Khartoum on its part has been obstructing resolution of the Abyei situation. It is time for the people of Abyei to be saved from their own leaders.

Khartoum also needs to be helped to be brave enough to deal with the Messiria Baggara Arabs; and the Arabs need to be reassured by all sides that whatever the decision of the Ngok Dinka in their referendum they will always have grazing and watering rights at the River Kiir. The Abyei protocol is not clear on this, although it cannot be thought that, if Abyei ever reverted to South Sudan as a territory, the Baggara Arabs would be denied these rights. But as people seek to resolve such an intricate matter, it is always good to make reassurances.

Finally, all sides in this Abyei conflict need to tell the government of South Sudan that it is peace with Northern Sudan that they seek and nothing else. The Ngok people of Abyei have had enough, and surely their own children, who are the rulers of South Sudan, can use South Sudan's power to bring peace to their own people.

Khartoum and Juba have proved beyond reasonable doubt that neither of them wants to implement the Abyei protocol, because each of them fears that the implementation may bring a result that is not favourable to them. What if the majority of the Ngok people of Abyei do not want to return to the South and vote in the referendum to remain in the North? Would the Ngok leaders of the SPLM in Juba accept that? Those who are in charge of Abyei affairs within the SPLM do not believe that there are enough Ngok people of Abyei who want to remain in Northern Sudan. Yet, with the security, economic and administrative situation in South Sudan being what it is today, one must not rule out the unexpected occurring.

There remain a vocal number of Ngok people of Abyei who are strongly advocating that Abyei should remain part of Northern Sudan. Their abilities and power should not be underrated or ignored. And, of course, such a crucial vote must not be rigged.

There is a wider problem beyond Abyei which the international community should take responsibility for. This is the question of the demarcation of the border between the two states of Sudan. The assumption made that once they had signed the CPA Khartoum and Juba would cooperate in their own best interests and would implement the peace agreement in good faith has been proved wrong. This should mean, therefore, that the international community which orchestrated the CPA on behalf of the people of Sudan should step into the picture again to ensure that the outstanding items are implemented. The most important of these is the border demarcation. Without a signed border agreement between the two Sudans, threats of war between them will remain. And it is not just the threat of war, but the threat of livelihood for the people of the two Sudans.

The border between the two Sudans is one of the world's longest, nearly 2,000 miles. It is the type of border that can only be policed through mutually agreed demarcation. The basis for such demarcation, the provincial borders of the one Sudan, as they stood at the time of independence on 1 January 1956, is the only credible position on the borders between the two Sudans, especially considering that every-thing between these two Sudanese states is contested and the fact that it is clearly stated in the CPA as part of the peace agreement between the two that the borders between them are as they stood on 1 January 1956.

Yet there are obvious problems that need to be solved, even over the 1956 borders between Northern Sudan and South Sudan. This is because the North, which had been in effect the ruler of Sudan before South Sudan broke away from the union, had made unilateral adjust-ments of the common borders of 1956.

Two examples illustrate this phenomenon of border redemarcation between the South and the North without agreement. The first is Kafia Kenji, in the Western Bahr el Ghazal district of Raga. In 1960, a mere five years after Sudan became independent from Britain, the military head of the Sudanese state, General Ibrahim Abboud, decreed that Kafia Kenji would, from the day of that decree, become part of neighbouring Darfur to Bahr el Ghazal and would therefore be part of Northern Sudan. General Abboud did this because (as mentioned in earlier chapters) it was rumoured that geological surveyors had discovered uranium at the Kafia Kenji area. Not only did General Abboud decree that Kafia Kenji was now Northern Sudan, but he also had it renamed 'Hofrat el Nahas', the Arabic for the 'hole of copper'. New maps were very quickly prepared, showing Kafia Kenji of South Sudan as a new Northern Sudanese site called the 'hole of copper'. All efforts to return Hofrat el Nahas to South Sudan failed, even after a second military intervention, when General Jaafar Mohamed Nimeiri had granted South Sudan regional self-rule in 1972 and agreed to return Kafia Kenji to South Sudan. Khartoum continued to inspire and instigate the Northern Sudanese province of Darfur to insist that Kafia Kenji is a Northern Sudanese territory and that it is called Hofrat el Nahas, not Kafia Kenji.

On the Upper Nile borders of South Sudan with Northern Sudan, Khartoum had adjusted the vast fertile agricultural areas of Renk; Wad Akono, west of Renk; and Maban, north-east of Meluth and Renk. All these areas, which fall to South Sudan on the maps of 1956, are all now disputed border territories between Sudan and South Sudan. The vast mechanized agriculture schemes here are now almost exclusively farmed by Northern Sudanese. So far, however, the border lines between South Sudan and Northern Sudan have not been tampered with in this area and so, therefore, border demarcation may not become a problem here as it is elsewhere.

Members of the international community who helped Khartoum and Juba sign the CPA some ten years ago, now can hopefully assist the two countries in adjusting their common borders in accordance with the CPA and to finalize the demarcation of the border.

The six years during which South Sudan and Northern Sudan should have implemented all the provisions of the CPA before the South voted in its 2010 referendum were wasted, because the two parties spent the time accusing each other of failing to do their job. Khartoum was not prepared to do anything in South Sudan, as this would have been wasted effort if the South voted for independence in 2010. After all, one of the reasons for the South deciding to vote for independence was the long failure by the North to carry out any development in South Sudan.

However, for the leaders of the SPLM after Colonel Garang, the resources available for the development of South Sudan became their own individual private property and not for public services. The leaders of the SPLM argued that the responsibility for developing South Sudan and persuading the people of South Sudan to vote for unity with the North was with the North, and not with them. But these leaders were drawing 50 per cent of the oil revenue for themselves, while blaming the North for not developing the South.

Furthermore, the CPA required that while the SPLM had to be fully in charge of the affairs of South Sudan during the interim period, it had to occupy 50 per cent of state power in Khartoum, to ensure that some development by central government took place in South Sudan before the referendum on self-determination by the South. Instead, the SPLM leaders used their power in Khartoum to obstruct implementation of the CPA.

Clearly, the future of the peace agreement between the South and the North was affected by this obstructionist rather than constructive attitude, which both Sudanese signatories to the CPA should have adopted. But we are now where we are. If the regional and international community want to secure peace for South Sudan and between the two Sudans, it should now intervene to sort out the Abyei situation.

The Ngok Dinka people of Abyei must be enabled to carry out their referendum. It is not unreasonable to assume that the governments in Khartoum and Juba will never agree on anything, including all the protocols that have yet to be implemented. Since the international community oversaw the CPA, it should have an interest in ensuring that all the protocols of the CPA are implemented, in both spirit and letter, to the satisfaction of all parties concerned.

To this end, the two parties to the Abyei protocol of the CPA are behaving in an incredibly unruly way. It is impossible to believe that the SPLM leaders of the Abyei community could have imagined that they would put both Khartoum and Juba on the spot by conducting their own referendum without due process in 2013. How they could have thought that Juba and Khartoum would recognize such a move in which they had no hand is beyond belief. Perhaps they thought Juba would go along with the illegitimate referendum, having failed over the years to rein in the Ngok leaders of the SPLM. How otherwise could they have managed to obtain the funds, the transport and communications and other facilities to conduct their illegitimate referendum of 2013 without dipping into the coffers of the central government of South Sudan?

Now, those who may be thinking of resolving the problem of Abyei must be aware of what the Messiria Arabs will do if a legitimate referendum of the Ngok people of Abyei is conducted, and the people of Abyei decide to become citizens of South Sudan again. The Messiria Arabs are already threatening to retaliate if this takes place. Unless the international community ensures that Khartoum abides by the result of the Abyei referendum, this result might not make any difference to the people of Abyei in terms of their security. Already the Messiria Baggara Arabs are threatening to hold their own referendum as a counter to the CPA protocol.

The Abyei protocol clearly states that only the Ngok Dinka people of Abyei should decide on their future. This is not just a matter of ethnicity or culture, it is also a matter of history – which is why dates are quoted. The Ngok Dinka people of Abyei were part of South Sudan before their own leaders decided in 1905 to be part of Northern Sudan. It was unfortunate that this was about the same time that the British colonial powers were thinking about what to do with South Sudan. Annexing South Sudan to Northern Sudan, for instance, must have already been in their minds, so that placing the Ngok people in Northern Sudan may have become a useful test case. It has obviously not worked: South Sudan is now an independent country and the Ngok people of Abyei are not being well treated in the North. So, why not give them the opportunity, already legally accorded to them by the CPA, to decide whether or not they want to return to South Sudan? Clearly, the international community, particularly those who were the mediators and therefore guardians of the CPA, should ensure that the Abyei referendum should be implemented.

It should not be too difficult for the international community to find a reason to conduct the Abyei referendum rather than let it continue as a dispute between Khartoum and Juba. After all, the Khartoum and Juba governments have accepted the presence of a large UN peacekeeping force in South Sudan and in Northern Sudan. The force already has a strong presence in Abyei too. Indeed, it is the only security presence there at the time of this writing. All that is required is technical personnel to conduct the referendum.

Between them, the UN and the AU, represented by its Horn of Africa regional organization, IGAD, can easily conduct the referendum. The type of funding necessary to conduct it is surely not beyond the reach of the UN and the three countries of the troika.

Fulfilling the Abyei protocol should not be left to the government of South Sudan alone, as it is so dominated by Deng Majok Kuol Arop's children of the SPLM. Khartoum will not accept and cannot trust the outcome of such a procedure. The same would apply to Khartoum conducting the referendum on its own, even under the pretext that Abyei remains part of Northern Sudan according to the maps of 1 January 1956. If the Abyei referendum were conducted by the international community, this should compel the two governments to respect the outcome. This would not only be a fitting final implementation of the CPA, but it might also introduce a new sense of cooperation; this could normalize relations between the two countries. Nothing could be better than that for the people of Northern Sudan and South Sudan.

The Ngok people of Abyei have reached their current impasse because neither their leaders nor the leadership of South Sudan has been honest, or faced the reality and the truth of the Abyei situation. If they had, the resolution would have been possible some time ago. It was essential to draw the parameters of the problem in order to find a solution. This would have clearly indicated that the problem is social and not political. If it had been defined this way and confined to its proper parameters, a solution would have been possible. Instead, the political leaders of the Ngok Dinka aspired for a long time to make the case of the Ngok people synonymous with the political cause of South

Sudan. If the Abyei situation was not resolved then the situation of South Sudan would not be resolved either.

For a long time, the people of South Sudan had concluded that only war – a long civil war, or several of them for that matter – could bring resolution to the South's dispute with the North. In the end, history proved that this unspoken view was correct – and they won their freedom from the North after a very long armed struggle.

Throughout this struggle, the Ngok people of Abyei were not totally absent, at least as far as the leadership of the South Sudanese political movement was concerned. But today their leadership of the Sudan People's Liberation Movement is now engrossed in political disagreements in a ruling political party that has showed no concern or interest in the ordinary people of South Sudan. These leaders in the ruling party of South Sudan, the SPLM, are merely exploiting the current situation. Not only have the leaders of the Ngok people of the SPLM neglected their duty towards their own people, but they are now part of the power struggle within South Sudan, before securing the return of the Ngok people of Abyei to South Sudan.

Therefore, the case of the Ngok people of Abyei now hangs in the balance, outside the framework of an independent South Sudan. There are now many people in South Sudan who feel that if this is the way the Ngok leaders are behaving in the politics of South Sudan before they even join South Sudan properly, then it is better for South Sudan to stop trying to negotiate for the return of the Ngok Dinka people of Abyei from Northern Sudan.

It was South Sudan that proposed in March 1965, at the Round Table Conference in Khartoum, that the borders demarcated by the British colonial authorities for the nine provinces of Sudan before independence should be respected. Abyei at that point was already part of Northern Sudan. It remains so until its people can speak in their referendum. Until that happens, anything that the leaders of the SPLM from Abyei are doing about Abyei, including exercising power in the government of South Sudan, on behalf of the people of South Sudan, is not legitimate.

In the end, the case of Abyei can only finally be resolved when the leadership in Juba and Khartoum normalize their relations and get together to find a solution, not as a political problem, but as a social problem that affects people in a small area and will not seriously affect the socio-political situation either in South Sudan or in Northern Sudan.

Apart from addressing the situation that prevails between Juba and Khartoum today, what should happen to the Messiria Baggara Arabs and their cattle has to be considered, once the Ngok people of Abyei have decided in their legitimate plebiscite under the CPA to revert back to South Sudan. What will happen to the Baggara Arabs if Abyei and the part of the River Kiir that belongs to Abyei, and by extension therefore now belongs to Southern Kordofan and to Northern Sudan, returns to the South? If Khartoum and Juba enjoyed normal relations they should not find it too difficult to resolve this issue. Even the tribal chiefs of the Sudan native administration found an easy solution to these grazing problems when there was a credible native administration during the colonial period. What the people in the Abyei area of Southern Kordofan are suffering from is the failure of politics in both Khartoum and Juba to resolve this essentially straightforward matter. What a terrible shame!

Bibliography

Ahmed, Abdel Ghaffar M. and Sorbo, Gunnar M., S*udan Divided: Continuing Conflict in a Contested State*. New York: Palgrave Macmillan, 2013.

Akol, Lam, *S.P.L.M./S.P.L.A.: Inside an African Revolution*. Khartoum: Khartoum University Printing Press, 2009.

Alford, Henry Stamford Lewis and Dennistoun Sword, W., *The Egyptian Soudan: Its Loss and Recovery*. London: Macmillan and Co. Ltd., 1898.

Ali, Abbas Ibrahim Muhammad, *The British, the Slave Trade, and Slavery in the Sudan, 1820–1881*. Khartoum: Khartoum University Press, 1972.

Beswick, Stephanie, *Sudan's Blood Memory: The Legacy of War, Ethnicity, and Slavery in Early South Sudan*. Rochester, NY: University of Rochester Press, 2004.

Both, Peter, *South Sudan: Forgotten Tragedy*. Bloomington, IN: 1st Books Library, 2003.

Colson, Audrey Butt, *The Nilotes of the Sudan and Uganda*. London: International African Institute, 1964.

Dempsey, James, *Mission on the Nile*. London: Burns & Oates, 1955.

Divisions in Sudan's Ruling Party and the Threat to the Country's Future Stability. Brussels : International Crisis Group, 2011.

Evans-Pritchard, E.E., *Les Nuer: Description des modes de vie et des institutions politiques d'un peuple nilote*. Translated by Louis Dumont. Paris: Gallimard, 1968.

Grandin, Nicole, *Le Soudan Nilotique et l'administration Britannique (1898–1956)*. Leiden: E.J. Brill, 1982.

Grawert, Elke (ed.), *After the Comprehensive Peace Agreement in Sudan*. Rochester, NY: James Currey, 2010.

Hartley, Paul F. and Bland, Robert (eds.), *South Sudan: Challenges and Opportunities for Africa's New Nation*. New York: Nova Science Publishers Inc., 2012.

Hosti, Christop et al., *Southern Sudan*. Bern: University of Bern, 2008.

Jackson, Nicholas A., *Southern Sudanese Independence Referendum, 2011*. Washington, DC: Congressional Cartography Program, 2011.

James, Wendy. *War and Survival in Sudan's Frontierlands: Voices from the Blue Nile*. Oxford: Oxford University Press, 2007.

Kadouf, Hunud Abia, *An Outline of Dinka Customary Law in the Jonglei Area*. Khartoum: 1977.

LeRiche, Matthew, *South Sudan: From Revolution to Independence*. London: Hurst, 2012.

Lienhardt, R.G., *Divinity and Experience: The Religion of the Dinka*. Oxford: Clarendon Press, 1961.

Madut, Chan Reech, *Some Aspects of Bridewealth among the Dinka with Special Reference to the Twich Dinka of Kongor District, South Sudan*. Khartoum: 1984.

Madut-Kuendit, Lewis Anei, *The Dinka History, the Ancients of Sudan: From Abuk and Garang to the Present Day Dinka*. Kampala: Mignit Technologies Ltd., 2010.

Makec, John Wuol, *The Customary Law of the Dinka (Jieng): A Comparative Analysis of an African Legal System*. Khartoum: St George Printing Press, 1986.

Makec, John Wuol, *The Customary Law of the Dinka People of Sudan: In Comparison with Aspects of Western and Islamic Laws*. London: Afroworld Publishing Co., 1988.

Malwal, Bona, *The Sudan: A Second Challenge to Nationhood*. New York: Thornton Books, 1985.

Malwal, Bona, *The Comprehensive Peace Agreement 2005: A Critique*. Omdurman, Sudan: Abdel Karim Mirghani Cultural Centre, 2005.

Malwal, Bona, *Sudan and South Sudan: From One to Two*. Basingstoke: Palgrave Macmillan, 2015.

Martin, Percy F., *The Sudan in Evolution: A Study of the Economic, Financial, and Administrative Conditions of the Anglo-Egyptian Sudan*. London: Constable & Co. Ltd., 1921.

Takpany, Martin Marial, *Curriculum Development in the Southern Sudan and the Problems of Educational Planning.* Juba: University of Juba, 1985.

The Addis Ababa Agreement and the Problem of the South Sudan, as Amended by the South Sudan Liberation Movement.

Zainelabdin, Amin, *Abyei: Origins of the Conflict and the Question of Arbitration.* Beltsville, MD: International Graphics, 2011.

Index